B S C S

THE
Nature of Science
AND THE STUDY OF
Biological Evolution

BSCS

5415 Mark Dabling Blvd., Colorado Springs, CO 80918-3842 USA

www.BSCS.org

Acknowledgments

BSCS Administrative Staff

Carlo Parravano, *Chair, Board of Directors*
Rodger W. Bybee, *Executive Director*
Janet Carlson Powell, *Associate Director*
Pamela Van Scotter, *Director, Center for Curriculum Development*
Marcia Mitchell, *Director of Finance*

BSCS Project Team

Rodger W. Bybee, *Principal Investigator*
David A. Hanych, *Project Director*
Hedi Baxter, *Curriculum Developer*
April Gardner, *Curriculum Developer*
Wendy Haggren, *Curriculum Developer*
Nicole Knapp, *Research Assistant*
Ted Lamb, *Evaluator*
Stephen Pasquale, *Curriculum Developer*
Terry Redmond, *Administrative Assistant*
Anne Westbrook, *Curriculum Developer*
Carrie Zander, *Administrative Assistant*

BSCS Production Department

Barbara Perrin, *Creative Director*
Barbara Resch, *Editor*
Stacey Luce, *Production Specialist*

MW Productions Multimedia Developer,
    Doug Weihnacht
Peaceful Solutions Graphic Design, *Rick Bickhart*

Advisory Committee

Garland Allen, Washington University, St. Louis, Missouri
John Beatty, University of Minnesota, St. Paul, Minnesota
Kenneth Bingman, Blue Valley West High School,
    Stilwell, Kansas
Timothy Goldsmith, Yale University, New Haven, Connecticut
Barbara Grosz, Pine Crest High School,
    Fort Lauderdale, Florida
Jon Herron, University of Washington, Seattle, Washington
Norman Lederman, Illinois Institute of Technology,
    Chicago, Illinois
Cynthia Mannix, The Bishop School, La Jolla, California
John Moore, University of California, Riverside
M. Patricia Morse, University of Washington,
    Seattle, Washington
John Settlage, University of Utah, Salt Lake City, Utah
John Spengler, Pine Creek High School,
    Colorado Springs, Colorado

Educational Consultants

Sam Donovan, University of Pittsburgh,
    Pittsburgh, Pennsylvania
Susan Mazer, University of California,
    Santa Barbara, California
Lynda Micikas, Denver Christian High School,
    Denver, Colorado

Contributing Writers

Edward Drexler, Pius XI High School, Milwaukee, Wisconsin
Barbara Grosz, Pine Crest High School,
    Fort Lauderdale, Florida
Brett Merritt, Okemos Public Schools, Okemos, Michigan
Lynda Micikas, Denver Christian High School,
    Denver, Colorado

Pilot-Test Teachers

Kenneth Bingman, Blue Valley West High School,
    Stilwell, Kansas
Doug Lundberg, Air Academy High School,
    Colorado Springs, Colorado
Lynda Micikas, Denver Christian High School,
    Denver, Colorado
John Spengler, Pine Creek High School,
    Colorado Springs, Colorado

Field-Test Teachers

Penny Antkowiak, Deer Creek High School,
    Edmond, Oklahoma
Lindsay Bacall, Windsor High School, Windsor, Connecticut
John Bayerl, Dearborn Fordson High School,
    Dearborn, Michigan
Ann Campbell, Legacy High School, Broomfield, Colorado
Julie Cunningham, Clintonville High School,
    Clintonville, Wisconsin
Christine Grant, Warren Mott High School, Warren, Michigan
Sharon Harter, Coronado High School,
    Colorado Springs, Colorado
Elizabeth Hickey, Cocoa High School, Cocoa, Florida
Jerrie Mallicoat, Titusville High School, Titusville, Florida
James Meegan, Melbourne High School, Melbourne, Florida
Judith Nuno, Marymount High School,
    Los Angeles, California
Jim Ramsey, Kamiakin High School, Kennewick, Washington
Tammy Rickard, Spain Park High School,
    Birmingham, Alabama
John Spengler, Pine Creek High School,
    Colorado Springs, Colorado

1-929614-19-5

This material is based on work supported by the National Science Foundation under Grant No. ESI-0099181.

Any opinions, findings, conclusions, or recommendations expressed in this publication are those of the authors and do not necessarily reflect the view of the granting agency.

Cover and interior design: Rick Bickhart

Dedication

This book is dedicated to the memory of

John A. Moore.

Teachers and students have had a richer science education

due to the tireless efforts of this great biologist.

John A. Moore championed the teaching of the nature of science

and biological evolution for 45 years. Dr. Moore was among the

biologists who developed the first BSCS textbooks in the

late 1950s, and he was an advisor for this book.

Color Key

Text in the following colors indicates:

■ **Quote**

■ **Key Idea**

■ **Zoom In**

■ **Take Charge of Your Learning**

■ **Highlight *and* Activity**

Contents

Ways of
Knowing Life

Chapter 1

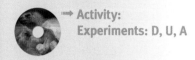

➡ Activity:
Experiments: D, U, A

You step onto an airplane for an overseas flight and notice most of the people are wearing surgical masks. What has happened? An accident? A terrorist attack? You are surprised to learn that they are taking precautions against a deadly, new, naturally occurring disease.

Eerie scenes like this occurred in 2003 as a dangerous respiratory disease called severe acute respiratory syndrome (SARS) began to kill people. Rapid scientific investigation identified the cause: a virus spread to people in distant locations by air travelers. Precautions such as the masks, frequent hand washing, and isolation of sick people helped to contain the initial outbreak.

How do new diseases arise? Often, diseases occur when a genetic change in a virus or bacterial population lets it infect new hosts or cause more damage. The changes could occur in the hosts themselves. In some cases, humans unintentionally encourage new threats of infection by overusing bacterial antibiotics. Widespread use of penicillin, for example, was an effective pressure to increase the number of disease-causing bacteria that could resist the antibiotic.

Living systems are constantly changing—new strains are gradually produced, and the new interactions occur. Look carefully at the life around you. How are the organisms around you different from one another? How are they the same? How are they suited to their surroundings?

Diversity, Unity, and Adaptation

If you look closely at life on Earth, you'll notice how diverse it is. No matter where you live, Earth is inhabited by a dazzling variety of life. Towering trees, tiny bacteria, colorful flowers, foul-smelling mushrooms, soaring birds, slimy earthworms, buzzing insects, and curious humans. Living things come in an astonishing variety of sizes, shapes, colors, and lifestyles.

People have benefited from the diversity of life for thousands of years. It affects how we live, what we eat, what we wear, and what we do for fun. The world's living things are a source of food, medicine, and building materials. They also play an important role in recycling nutrients, regulating climate, and purifying wastes. And they make the world a more interesting and beautiful place to live. Try to imagine a world without flowers, trees, whales, mushrooms, or elephants. Someone once said that if all the world's creatures disappeared, humans would feel a great loneliness. More accurately, humans most likely would not survive.

Considering extremes is one way to grasp the range of diversity. For example, do you know which species is the largest and which is the smallest? Which has the longest life span and which has the shortest? Which lives in the hottest environments and which in the coldest? Look at the following pictures to discover the answers to these questions and more.

*Life occurs in astonishing variety. The largest of the large—a blue whale, Balaenoptera musculus (**a**) and a redwood tree, Sequoia sempervirens (**b**). The smallest of the small—bacteria (**c**). Some adult mayflies, Ephemeroptera, (**d**) live only a few hours, whereas bristlecone pines, Pinus longaeva, (**e**) can live for thousands of years. Heat-loving bacteria like Thermus aquaticus (**f**) live in hot-temperature springs; cylindroeystis breissonii (green algae) (**g**) lives in snow on high mountains.*

Now look at the table on the following page. What organisms make up most of the world's known species? How many are estimated to exist? How many did you expect? Think about the many unusual or bizarre traits organisms possess. Who would ever imagine a flower that looks like a bee? And why are some frogs so brightly colored?

Biological scientists have discovered that although life on Earth is amazingly diverse, it also shows remarkable unity. The world's species have many traits in common. Scientists also have discovered that many of the traits organisms possess, even those that seem odd or bizarre, adapt them to their environment. Let's look at what scientists know about the diversity, the unity, and the adaptations of life.

Type of Organism*	Number of Described Species (%)	Estimated Number of Species (%)**
Arthropods	1,065,000 (61%)	8,900,000 (65%)
Land Plants	270,000 (15%)	320,000 (2%)
Protoctists	80,000 (5%)	600,000 (4%)
Fungi	72,000 (4%)	1,500,000 (11%)
Molluscs	70,000 (4%)	200,000 (1%)
Chordates	45,000 (3%)	50,000 (< 1%)
Mewatodes	25,000 (1%)	400,000 (3%)
Bacteria	4,000 (< 1%)	1,000,000 (7%)
Viruses	4,000 (< 1%)	400,000 (3%)
Other	115,000 (7%)	250,000 (2%)
Total	**1,750,000 (100%)**	**13,620,000 (98%)**

Note: *The majority of described species are arthropods, which includes the insects. Scientists estimate that 13 million or more species actually exist.*
*Viruses are included as part of Earth's diversity even though some scientists do not consider them to be living organisms.
**The percentages do not add up to 100 percent because of rounding.*

Millions of species inhabit Earth.

Diversity

Scientists use the term *diversity* to describe the variety of living things they have observed in the world. Diversity sometimes refers to the diverse sizes, shapes, colors, behaviors, and lifestyles of organisms. It also can refer to the number of species that inhabit Earth. As you have seen, scientists have currently identified and at least partially described approximately 1.75 million species. Discoveries increase the number of known species constantly.

Although scientists have discovered nearly 2 million species, they estimate that many more exist. At least 13 million species are thought to inhabit Earth, maybe more. Many of these undiscovered species live in the tropics. In fact, scientists estimate they have identified only about 10 percent of the species that live in the tropics and know very little about them.

How did the diversity of life arise? This question has intrigued people for thousands of years. In the next chapter, you will learn how the biological explanation of diversity was built on a foundation of scientific evidence.

Unity

If you continue to look closely at the diversity of life, you'll notice that all species, no matter how different they are, share certain traits. For example, all living things are made of one or more cells. The cell is the basic structural and functional unit of life. All animals, plants, fungi, protozoans, and bacteria are made of cells.

Scientists use the term unity to refer to the observation that all living things share certain key traits. For example, if you look at the activity inside cells, you find that all cells have certain chemical reactions in common. For instance, all cells build up and break down ATP, the molecule that stores energy in the body for powering chemical reactions.

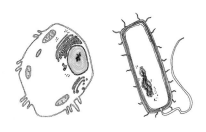

All organisms are made of cells. Eukaryotic cells (left) contain membrane-enclosed organelles such as a nucleus; prokaryotic cells (right) do not. Plants, animals, fungi, and protozoans are composed of eukaryotic cells. Bacteria are prokaryotic cells.

If you look still deeper, you will encounter the most striking unifying characteristics of all—DNA and RNA, the molecules that carry the genetic code. DNA provides the means by which all cellular organisms pass their traits to the next generation. Viruses use DNA or RNA for that role. Genes in the DNA also direct the functioning of cells.

Both ancient and modern life-forms show the unity of life. Bacteria, for example, are the oldest life-form on Earth. Despite the great time span, the bacteria that lived 2 billion years ago look like bacteria living today. Bacteria encode their genetic information in DNA, and they synthesize proteins using the same basic mechanism as all other life-forms. When you focus on the unifying characteristics of life, you find that Earth's species are more alike than you might think.

So why do diverse organisms have certain traits in common?

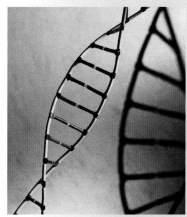

DNA is the genetic material in all organisms (except some viruses).

All species have certain traits in common.

Adaptation

Every species has traits that help suit it to its surroundings. When scientists refer to a species's *adaptations*, they are talking about specific traits that help individuals survive and reproduce in their native environment.

Adaptations include physical traits such as the particular shape, size, or color of a body structure. For example, the sphinx moth has a long feeding tube that it uses to reach the nectar buried deep within a flower. Likewise, a vampire bat has sharp front teeth that it uses to puncture the skin of a mammal. It then feeds by drinking some of the victim's blood.

The feeding tube–or proboscis–of a sphinx moth can be 20 centimeters (8 inches) or more in length (left). A vampire bat's bite is not very harmful, although the bat may transmit rabies or other diseases (right).

Adaptations also can be physiological and biochemical. For example, camels produce concentrated urine and very dry feces. These physiological adaptations help them conserve water in dry desert conditions. Some arthropods produce a chemical antifreeze prior to overwintering. How might the production of this chemical be adaptive?

Behaviors can be adaptive too. For example, male and female monarch butterflies begin mating on the ground, but the male then carries the female to a tree where mating continues. How might this behavior promote survival and reproduction? How might you test your idea?

Camels (left) are adapted to life in the desert. Male and female monarch butterflies at overwintering sites in California and Mexico begin mating on the ground (right), but then fly to a nearby tree.

Asking Questions about Diversity, Unity, and Adaptation

Some of the most interesting and challenging questions biologists have tackled are ones about diversity, unity, and adaptation. For example, when and how did species originate? How does a species acquire adaptations helpful in its environment? Why do all living things share a common set of traits?

Asking and answering questions about life, describing and explaining the things around us, and communicating what we know to others are fundamental human activities. People have done this throughout recorded history. Why? It's a hard question to answer, but perhaps it is because humans are naturally curious. Biologist E. O. Wilson called our curiosity about life biophilia, the love of life. Or perhaps it is because coming to know the world around us is a way of coming to know ourselves. In the rest of this chapter, you will explore some of the different ways people have come to know the natural world and explain what they have observed. You will also learn how scientific explanations are built.

Species have traits that promote individual survival and reproduction.

"The diversity and unity of life are equally striking and meaningful aspects of the living world."

Theodosius Dobzhansky, biologist

Knowing the Natural World

Look around the world. It is a challenging task to understand and accurately describe natural processes and even to use these principles to build things like computers, automobiles, or medicines. How much do you understand about the natural things around you? What do you know about lightning, volcanoes, viruses, or elephants? What about the stars, the planets, and black holes?

Consider a small cluster of stars known to modern astronomers as Messier Object 45 (or M45). It is found in the constellation Taurus, the bull. The cluster contains some gaseous material and several thousand stars, but only a few of them are visible to the naked eye.

In the image of the constellations Taurus and Orion, star cluster M45 is found near the middle.

How have people come to know these stars across history? The earliest evidence of people's awareness of M45 may be an image painted 16,500 years ago on the wall of Lascaux Cave in France. In the painting, a group of dots appears above a bull's neck. The pattern of dots bears a striking resemblance to the pattern of stars visible in M45. Was this cave painting an early description of this star cluster? What kind of information would you need to collect to help you answer this question?

More than 2,000 years ago, the ancient Greeks named this star cluster for the seven mythical daughters of the gods Atlas and

The Dance of the Pleiades *by Elihu Vedder*

Pleione. They called it the Pleiades, or the Seven Sisters, and named the individual stars after the daughters. We still use these names today when referring to the visible stars in the cluster. People typically see only six stars when they observe the Pleiades with the naked eye.

How did the Greeks explain the origin of this cluster? According to Greek legend, the hunter Orion liked to chase the seven sisters on Earth even though he could not catch them. To end the chase, the god Zeus placed them in the heavens as stars. There, the constellation Orion continues the pursuit, never successful but always persistent.

Has our knowledge of this cluster and its origin changed across time? Yes! For example, in the early 1600s, people invented a new piece of technology called a telescope. An early scientist named Galileo used this technology to make some observations that changed people's understanding of the heavens, including the Pleiades. He discovered that the Pleiades and other parts of the sky contain more stars than anyone had ever imagined.

To expand people's understanding of the heavens, Galileo used a scientific approach to study something that was already well known to people. He carefully observed the area of the sky where the Pleiades were located with his telescope and recorded the number and pattern of stars he saw. Using these data as evidence, he concluded that the sky contained more stars than people could see with the naked eye. He then communicated his findings in a book titled *Sidereus Nuncius* (*The Sidereal Messenger*) in 1610. By publishing his observations, Galileo presented his evidence to the public for review and verification.

Galileo purposely chose the Pleiades, a well-known group of stars, to illustrate that the sky contained more stars than people could see with the naked eye. In the years that followed, people tested and confirmed Galileo's findings by looking at the Pleiades and other parts of the sky. For example, Galileo saw more than 40 stars in the cluster. In 1644, scientists using a larger telescope counted 78 stars. By the 1870s, scientists had counted more than 600. Since then, scientists using even more powerful telescopes have observed more than 3,000 stars in the cluster. Furthermore, people have verified that other parts of the sky also contain many more stars than can be seen with the naked eye.

Careful scientific investigation has shown that the Pleiades star cluster is moving through a cloud of hydrogen gas and dust called

Scientists using an early telescope (insert); a modern research telescope

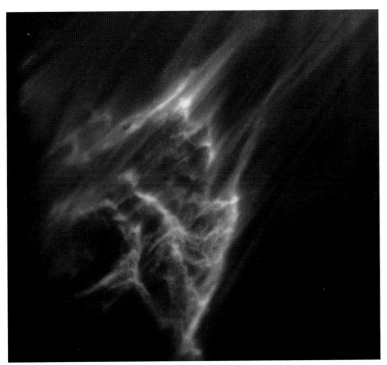

The Hubble Space Telescope provides a detailed view of the nebula described by Tennyson as a "silver braid."

a nebula. An image from the Hubble Space Telescope provides a detailed view of the nebula.

How do scientists know that the cluster is moving through a nebula? Measurements show that the nebula's rotation is different from that of the Pleiades stars. This rotational difference suggests that the star cluster is not part of the nebula, but simply moving through it.

How does modern science explain the origin of the Pleiades star cluster? Take charge of your learning and find out. Go to the library or the Internet and look for information on how science explains the origin of the Pleiades and other star clusters. Be ready to discuss your findings.

Why have both ancient and modern people studied and described this star cluster and tried to explain its existence? Perhaps they were inspired by its beauty, or driven by curiosity, or both. How humans feel is important, and what piques their curiosity can drive people to investigate the natural world.

Although scientific study has improved our understanding of the Pleiades, it has not lessened our fascination with it. Nor has it reduced the pleasure we feel at its beauty. More than 200 years after Galileo, the English poet Alfred, Lord Tennyson wrote,

Scientists rely on technology to gather data. New tools and techniques provide new evidence that guides scientific inquiry and advances scientific understanding. The accuracy of the data, and therefore the quality of an exploration, depends on the technology scientists use.

Many a night I saw the Pleiades,
rising thro' the mellow shade,
glitter like a swarm of fireflies
tangled in a silver braid.

Today, we know that the "silver braid" in Tennyson's poem is the nebula through which the star cluster is moving. Science helps us "know" the Pleiades in a physical sense. Greek myths and Tennyson's poem help us "know" it in a cultural and an aesthetic sense.

What will you see the next time you look up at the Pleiades? Will you see a cloud of interstellar gas and dust surrounding what we know to be several thousand stars? Or will you imagine the Seven Sisters fleeing Orion?

Science is one way of knowing the world.

Science as a Way of Knowing

In the previous section, we described several ways people have considered one small cluster of stars. Throughout history, people have developed different approaches to interact with the world and to express themselves. In other words, there are different ways to know things.

A way of knowing is a method or process that humans use to understand objects and events in the world. Painters, for example, need to "know," or understand the objects they wish to portray. Part of their work involves technical knowledge about light, color, and perspective, while part is an emotional and creative process to communicate a particular way of feeling. Writers work hard to understand the motives of people and events and to evoke emotions in their stories and poetry.

Looking at and responding to art is one way people try to understand—or know—what the artist knew and wanted to communicate. The French novelist Marcel Proust once said, "Only through art can we get outside of ourselves and know another's view of the universe. … Thanks to art, instead of seeing a single world, our own, we see it multiply until we have before us as many worlds as there are original artists." Art can be a powerful way of knowing certain aspects of the world for both the artist and the observer.

A painting by Paul Cézanne. Cézanne believed that to capture a moment of time in paint, an artist must "become" that moment and paint what she or he sees.

For asking questions about the natural world, a particularly disciplined approach has developed: science. It does not rely on opinion but on testable explanations and evidence. It does not deal with nonrational or supernatural concepts. In *Science as a Way of Knowing*, John Moore describes the basic assumption of natural sciences in the following way: "Nature is, in principle, knowable and its phenomena are assumed to have constant cause-effect relationships." Because science requires ongoing testing of its assumptions, it is self-correcting. Moore states that the result "is that science is the most powerful mechanism we have for obtaining confirmable information about the natural world."

Natural sciences, for example, focus on the *natural world—* that is, the matter, energy, and processes that make up the physical universe. Natural sciences usually inquire about how physical and living systems function. Biology, geology, and physics are examples of natural sciences. The social sciences, such as history, focus instead on the activities of humans. Historians collect and interpret data about past events and ideas, and people and their times, in an attempt to understand why and how past events occurred.

Evolutionary biology is a science that focuses on how species change across time. This focus on the history of life makes evolution, in part, a historical science. Historical sciences use clues from the past and present to infer the course of past events. Evolutionary biology also is an observational and experimental science that examines current evolutionary changes in populations.

Science has particular ways of learning about and understanding the world. Scientists observe the world; ask questions about it; design and conduct investigations; use technology and techniques to collect, analyze, and interpret data; develop descriptions, explanations, predictions, and models based on evidence; and communicate their procedures and conclusions to others through books, journal articles, or lectures for review and evaluation. Scientists evaluate each other's work by reviewing experimental procedures, examining evidence, identifying faulty reasoning, and suggesting alternative explanations.

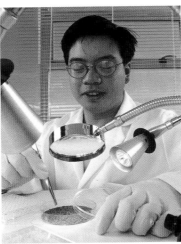
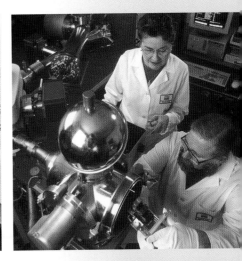

Science distinguishes itself from other ways of knowing through the use of verifiable observations, logical reasoning, and critical evaluation.

Zoom in for a closer look at scientific investigation.

Different kinds of questions call for different kinds of investigations. Some investigations involve observing and describing objects, organisms, or events; others involve collecting specimens; still others involve experiments in which scientists set up carefully designed tests to get evidence about a specific process or event. Computer models are one example of a scientific test. Current knowledge and understanding provide a starting point for scientific investigations. Investigations collect evidence or data that is compared with existing or new explanations. These investigations sometimes result in new ideas and new methods or procedures or techniques, and usually lead to new investigations.

Science is a human activity conducted by women and men of different social and ethnic backgrounds. Some scientists work in teams, while others work alone. All scientists rely on reasoning, insight, skill, and creativity to do their work. They also rely on certain habits of mind such as intellectual honesty, skepticism, and openness to new ideas.

People investigate the world scientifically because it provides powerful insights. The requirement for evidence and rational thinking has made scientific knowledge useful and generally durable. Because it keeps getting adjusted to reflect new evidence, it keeps getting more accurate. In the next section, we look at some of the characteristics of scientific explanations.

The Characteristics of Scientific Explanations

What characteristics of scientific explanations make them so powerful in describing natural phenomena?

- Scientific explanations are based on *empirical evidence.*
  Empirical evidence is information collected through our five senses—sight, hearing, smell, touch, and taste—with or without the aid of technology. For example, seeing a bird provides empirical evidence that it exists. This evidence-based approach is different from just relying on the opinions of famous authorities.

  Scientists gather information by making observations and conducting experiments. They sometimes use technology to extend their senses. Telescopes, for example, allow people to see distant objects more clearly. All science, whether it uses technology or not, is based on observations. Advances in scientific knowledge and understanding are based on observations that can be verified by other observers. Scientific explanations are not based on hunches or unsupported speculation.

Observations that have been repeatedly verified by others are accepted as facts. Observations may improve as technology improves. Accepted facts may change if it becomes possible to make more accurate observations.

■ **Scientific explanations are *testable*.** Scientists collect evidence that can support or refute explanations. Scientists test explanations by making additional observations and conducting experiments. Science cannot prove that a proposed explanation is correct with absolute certainty, but it can show that it is false. As physicist Albert Einstein pointed out, no amount of supporting evidence can guarantee that an explanation is correct because the next observation or experiment might produce refuting evidence. One valid piece of refuting evidence shows that all or more likely part of an explanation must be modified or refined.

> "No amount of experiments can ever prove me right; a single experiment may at any time prove me wrong."
>
> *Albert Einstein,*
> *Nobel Prize-winning physicist*

Science does not address issues that cannot be tested. Scientists may speculate, but their speculations are not accepted as scientific knowledge unless they can be posed as testable hypotheses and investigated scientifically.

A proposed or tentative explanation is also called a hypothesis. Scientists form hypotheses to help them direct their investigations. A **hypothesis** is a testable statement about the world. Scientists test a hypothesis by checking to see if its predictions are correct.

A **prediction** is a statement that follows logically from a hypothesis. For example, if hypothesis X leads you to make prediction Y, then you should be able to collect evidence that confirms or refutes prediction Y. Scientists make additional observations or conduct experiments to see if their predictions are confirmed (supported). If a prediction is confirmed, then the hypothesis gains support. If a prediction is refuted (proven false), then all or part of the hypothesis must be revised. Sometimes, tests do not fully confirm or refute a hypothesis and more tests are required.

Zoom in on scientific inquiry.

■ **Scientific explanations are open to change.** Scientific explanations are subject to improvement in light of new evidence. A scientific explanation is accepted as valid as long as it continues to pass all the tests scientists conduct. If an explanation fails a test of new evidence or reasoning, it is revised. Rarely is an existing explanation completely rejected, because scientific explanations are built on so much evidence to begin with.

Comprehensive and extensively tested explanations may be called theories. For example, the kinetic theory of matter explains temperature and pressure by proposing that matter is made up of tiny particles that are in constant motion. This explanation was first proposed in the 1600s and has been tested by hundreds of scientists. The theory explains the behavior of matter so well that essentially nearly all scientists today accept it. The theory of gravity and the cell theory of living systems are also fundamentally accepted explanations.

Most major ideas in science are supported by a lot of evidence, so they are not likely to change greatly in the future. In new areas where there is limited experimental or observational evidence, scientists may disagree over the interpretation of data. When this happens, they work towards finding evidence that resolves the disagreement.

TAKE CHARGE
OF YOUR LEARNING

As you learn how science investigates life on Earth, begin thinking and talking like a scientist. Be prepared to make observations, ask questions, construct hypotheses, make predictions, think of ways to test your hypotheses, and use terms in science correctly.

Thus, scientific explanations must be logical and consistent with multiple examples of observational or experimental evidence. To test tentative explanations (hypotheses), scientists make predictions based on the explanation and see if empirical evidence fits. Scientific explanations are open to criticism and modification and are communicated to the public. For other scientists and the general public to evaluate an explanation, scientists must report their methods, procedures, data, and conclusions.

As you have just seen, scientific explanations have certain characteristics. When people think about the world scientifically, they look for logical explanations that meet the requirements of science. Explanations of the natural world based on myths, personal beliefs, religious values, mystical inspiration, superstition, or supernatural events may be personally and socially important, but they are not scientific.

Be aware that nonscientists think scientifically all the time. For example, when you take your car to a repair shop to fix a problem for which there is no obvious cause, mechanics will usually solve the problem by thinking scientifically. They will make some observations about your car, ask themselves questions about what they observe, propose tentative explanations for the problem, test their explanations by making certain repairs, revise their explanations in light of new evidence about how your car runs, and eventually draw conclusions about the problem with your car.

Also be aware that scientists do not think scientifically about every aspect of their lives. For example, they may also produce art, and many scientists have deep religious faiths. But if their explanations of the natural world are to become part of the body of scientific knowledge, they must "think like a scientist" about those particular explanations.

The Meaning of the Word "Theory" in Science

A challenge facing both scientists and nonscientists is that people sometimes use different definitions for the same word. For example, think about the definition of the word "fact." To many nonscientists, a fact is something that is absolutely true. Scientists, however, do not think this way. To a scientist, a fact is an observation that is generally agreed upon. It is agreed upon because the observation has been made many times by many observers, using the best technology available. Scientists trust the facts they work with because they are confident that the facts are as correct as possible at the time. However, they know that facts can change as more accurate observations are made.

How do you react when you hear that the explanations of some issue have changed? Scientists are interested when they hear such news because they know that research continues to make more accurate observations. Nonscientists, however, sometimes miss this excitement and assume that a changed explanation has little value. How can you help your friends and family recognize the importance of changes in scientific knowledge?

Confusion also arises over the word "theory." To many nonscientists, a theory is a wild guess with little or no evidence to support it. To a scientist, a theory is *not* a guess. A theory is generally defined as an explanation that is firmly supported by evidence and widely accepted within the scientific community.

For example, the germ theory says that certain infectious diseases are caused by microorganisms. Prior to scientific investigation, many people believed that supernatural forces, poisonous vapors, or physiological imbalances caused such diseases. Scientists began collecting supporting evidence for the germ theory of disease during the 1800s. Today, most scientists and nonscientists accept the germ theory as the best supported explanation for infectious diseases.

To better understand the meaning of the word "theory" in science, let's look at how the germ theory of disease developed and changed. Our story begins in 1546, with a man named Girolamo Fracastoro. Fracastoro was an Italian doctor who studied infectious

Some Important Terms in Science

Observation
A specific piece of information gathered through the senses with or without the aid of technology. If you look at a flower and see that it is red, you have made an observation.

Fact
An observation that has been repeatedly verified by many observers. Facts are generally accepted as accurate.

Hypothesis
A tentative statement about the natural world such as a proposed explanation. A hypothesis leads to predictions that can be tested.

Prediction
A statement that follows logically from a hypothesis. Scientists test predictions by collecting data.

Theory
A comprehensive explanation of some aspect of the natural world that has been extensively tested and is widely accepted. Theories incorporate facts and confirmed hypotheses.

Source: Some Important Terms in Science table adapted from National Academy of Sciences. (1998). Teaching about evolution and the nature of science.

To scientists, a theory is a well-supported explanation.

Zoom in on how scientists and nonscientists use the word "theory."

diseases such as plague and syphilis. He published his ideas in a report titled *De contagione et contagiosis morbis (On Contagion and Contagious Diseases)*. He proposed that these diseases were caused by different types of tiny, rapidly multiplying "minute bodies" that were transferred from person to person through direct contact, by soiled clothing, and through the air. He based his explanation on a systematic study.

Fracastoro's hypothesis was widely praised when he published it, but it was soon forgotten. One problem was that the microscope had not yet been invented, so scientists did not have visual evidence that his minute bodies existed.

It wasn't until the 1800s that scientists began to accumulate direct evidence that supported Fracastoro's hypothesis. In 1835, Agostino Bassi demonstrated that a microscopic fungus caused a certain silkworm disease. In 1845, M. J. Berkeley showed that a fungus was responsible for Ireland's terrible potato blight. In 1865, the famous French scientist Louis Pasteur showed that a protozoan caused a different silkworm disease that almost destroyed the silk industry. His discovery helped save the industry.

As scientists began to understand the role of fungi and protozoans in causing disease, they wondered whether bacteria caused disease too. The first direct evidence that bacteria caused disease came in 1876. Robert Koch demonstrated a relationship between the disease anthrax and a bacterium called *Bacillus anthracis*. In 1884, Koch demonstrated beyond a reasonable doubt that the bacterium *Mycobacterium tuberculosis* caused tuberculosis. His research was so convincing that it motivated other scientists to

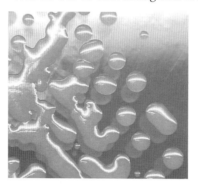

The bacteria that cause the disease anthrax.

begin studying infectious diseases. During the next 30 to 40 years, scientists identified the bacteria responsible for more than 20 such diseases, including cholera, pneumonia, whooping cough, and plague. All of this evidence strengthened the germ theory of disease.

So why is the germ theory called a theory? It's called a theory because it is not in doubt. By calling this explanation for infectious disease a theory, scientists are saying that it is supported by substantial evidence and widely accepted within the scientific community.

The Search for Answers Leads to More Questions

"Discovery is seeing what everybody else has seen and thinking what nobody else has thought."

Albert Szent-Gyorgi,
Nobel Prize-winning biologist

We began this chapter by considering some observations scientists have made about living things. These observations led them to ask many interesting and important questions, such as, How did so many different species originate? Why do they share certain traits? How did they become adapted to their environment?

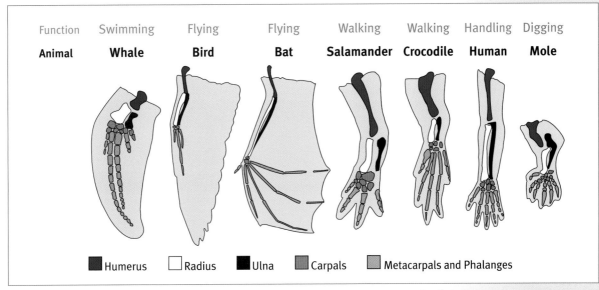

Function	Swimming	Flying	Flying	Walking	Walking	Handling	Digging
Animal	**Whale**	**Bird**	**Bat**	**Salamander**	**Crocodile**	**Human**	**Mole**

■ Humerus ☐ Radius ■ Ulna ▨ Carpals ▨ Metacarpals and Phalanges

Scientists have developed an explanation for diversity, unity, and adaptation that takes into account an enormous body of evidence about life on Earth. This explanation is called the theory of evolution. It qualifies as a theory because a large body of evidence supports it. In the next few chapters, you will examine this theory, how it was developed, and what evidence supports it.

Look at the shapes, patterns, and functions of the bones in the forelimbs of these animals. How do they illustrate diversity, unity, and adaptation? Be ready to discuss your answers.

As you learn about the theory of evolution, use your understanding of science as a way of knowing to analyze how scientists think. Remember that scientific explanations have important characteristics. Look for these characteristics in what you read. Keep in mind that because the theory of evolution is accepted as a fundamental principle of biology, it opens the door to many exciting areas of current research.

The theory of evolution is a comprehensive explanation for the diversity, unity, and adaptation of life. It is supported by a large body of evidence.

Recall also that science is a dynamic, collaborative, incremental, and cumulative way of learning about the world. Note how scientists continue to build upon the work of others by expanding, revising, and refining our understanding of evolution.

Activity:
Thinking like
a Scientist

Although the next few chapters focus on the search for answers to questions about life, keep in mind that searches always lead to new questions. As we saw in the story of the germ theory of disease, good scientific investigations often raise as many questions as they answer. Science thrives on the curiosity, passion, and energy of people who seek answers to important questions. Science benefits from the relentless probing of those who ask the next question, and the next, and the next.

Now once again, look carefully at the life around you. What do you see? What questions do your observations raise? ●

Charles Darwin and the Development of an Idea

Did you ever wonder why some people are great athletes or painters or musicians while others are exceptional carpenters or naturalists? Their life stories provide clues. By looking at Charles Darwin's life story, you will begin to understand how he was able to answer, in a scientifically convincing way, three of history's most baffling questions about diversity, unity, and adaptation: How do species form? Why do species have similar traits? and How do species become adapted to their surroundings?

In part, Darwin was able to answer these questions because his life experiences, interests, hobbies, friendships, knowledge, and personal qualities prepared him for a life of discovery. In this chapter, you will look first at Darwin's life story. You will then look to see what your life history is preparing you to do.

Begin your exploration by looking at the picture on this page. What ideas about science come to mind when you examine the picture? Be ready to discuss your interpretation. You will get another chance to interpret it after you finish the chapter.

Charles Darwin: Prepared for Discovery

Charles Darwin was born in England in 1809. In his autobiography, he described himself as "a very ordinary boy, rather below the common standard in intellect." In fact, his father once supposedly said to him, "You care for nothing but shooting, dogs, and rat-catching, and you will be a disgrace to yourself and all your family." Although Charles was an ordinary schoolboy, he received a good education, developed a strong interest in nature, and made extraordinary collections of pebbles, shells, eggs, insects, and other things from nature.

At the age of 16, Darwin entered the University of Edinburgh to study medicine and become a doctor like his father. His courses, however, did not interest him and the surgery he saw done on patients without painkillers nauseated him. Although Charles did not take his medical studies very seriously, he did continue to investigate nature and expand his collections. He also read widely, learned how to dissect organisms, skinned and stuffed birds, and presented reports at the local scientific society. Years later, these skills enabled him to collect evidence for a revolutionary idea and report it to the world.

It became clear after two years that Charles would never become a doctor, so his father suggested that he transfer to the University of Cambridge. There he would get a good general education that

Charles Darwin

TAKE CHARGE ●
OF YOUR LEARNING

As you read about Darwin's early life, list in your notebook the people, places, and events that prepared him for a life of scientific discovery. Be ready to discuss your list.

would prepare him to become a minister in the Anglican Church. Charles followed his advice. The idea of becoming a country minister and having time to pursue his interests in nature appealed to him. He did fairly well in his studies at Cambridge, but again spent much of his time outdoors in nature. He also developed a special fondness for collecting beetles.

Because of his keen interest in nature, Darwin became friends with several biology and geology professors at Cambridge and joined them on nature walks and field trips. He also read books on voyages of exploration. During this time, he developed a burning desire to explore the world and make some important discoveries of his own. Among those who recognized and appreciated Darwin's curiosity and knowledge about the living world was the professor of botany, John Henslow. Darwin often went out on field trips with this professor and became known as "the man who walks with Henslow." This teacher would soon play a critical role in Darwin's life.

What had Darwin had been taught, and what did he believe about diversity, unity, and adaptation? Like most scientists at the time, Darwin believed that each species had been created separately by God. This was not just a matter of faith or loyalty to the Bible, it seemed like a good explanation for what he saw in nature.

For example, if all species had been created by the same designer, it made sense that different species have some features in common. This is the same as buildings designed by the same architect having features in common. If a species had been created by a wise and kind designer, it also made sense that the members of each species have just the right features for surviving and reproducing in their particular environment. So the idea that all species had been created by a single, wise, and kind designer, namely God, seemed well supported by naturalists' observations.

This form of reasoning is known as natural theology. Natural theology is an attempt to explain nature in religious terms and to use observations of nature to support religious views. At the time Darwin was in school, scientists considered it the best way to explain the diversity, unity, and adaptations of life. Natural theology no longer counts as science, however, because it uses supernatural explanations. Later in the chapter, we will look more at the distinctions between natural and supernatural explanations, that is, explanations that are outside the realm of nature.

Darwin later gave up this viewpoint (at least partly). Why?

Zoom in for a closer look at Darwin's early life.

Because he made observations about nature that he found difficult to explain by supernatural processes but were better explained by natural processes. Explanations that use only observable processes of nature to account for what scientists observe are called naturalistic explanations. Before we get to those observations, however, let's look at how Darwin got the opportunity to make them.

Having just completed his degree at Cambridge and returned home, Darwin received a letter that changed his life. It invited him to sail around the world on a survey ship called the *Beagle*. He would be the ship's naturalist and a companion for the captain, Robert Fitz Roy. The captain needed a civilian companion because he was not allowed to be friends with the sailors under his command.

The survey ship Beagle

On the same day, Darwin also received a letter from his Cambridge teacher John Henslow. Henslow explained that he had been the one to recommend Darwin for the position. Henslow had recommended Darwin because he thought Charles was "the best qualified person I know of who is likely to undertake such a situation. I state this not on the supposition of your being a finished naturalist, but as amply qualified for collecting, observing, and noting anything worthy to be noted in natural history."

Charles wanted to accept the invitation, but he initially turned it down because his father objected. His father had many reasons for not wanting Charles to go on a two-year voyage aboard the *Beagle*. For one, sailors called ships designed like the *Beagle* "floating coffins" because they often sank in heavy seas. Also, the decks of the *Beagle* were rotting and had to be rebuilt. But mainly, Charles's father thought that it would be a waste of time and would not contribute to Charles's career.

Luckily, Charles's father had left a loophole. If Charles could find "any man of common sense" to recommend the trip, then his father would give him permission to go. Charles got the recommendation he needed from his uncle, a man his fathered respected, and became the *Beagle*'s naturalist. The stage was now set. Although Darwin didn't know it when he stepped aboard the *Beagle*, his observations and his explanation for those observations would forever change people's understanding of the natural world. Do you remember how scientists investigate the living world? If not, look back at Chapter 1.

Zoom in for a closer look at Robert Darwin's other objections to his son going on the *Beagle*.

The Voyage of the *Beagle*

The *Beagle* set sail from England in late 1831 when Charles was just 22 years old. It returned five long years later, not two years as planned.

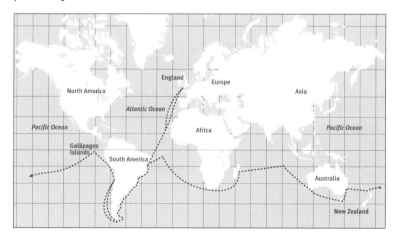

The Beagle *left England in December 1831. It explored the coasts of South America and the Galápagos Islands from February 1832 to October 1835. It reached Australia in January 1836 and the tip of Africa in May 1836, and arrived back in England in October 1836. How long did Darwin explore South America?*

Not only was the trip very long, it was also painful for Darwin, who suffered badly from seasickness. His cabin was small and he did not have much storage space for his belongings or his specimens. He and Captain Fitz Roy got along reasonably well, although they sometimes argued about details of religion and social practices such as slavery, which Darwin opposed.

Zoom in on Darwin's storage space on the *Beagle*.

Darwin was amazed by what he saw during the voyage. Some of his observations fit well with his previous understanding of the living world. For example, he saw an enormous diversity of species in the rain forests of South America. He wrote, "Delight is a weak term to express the feelings of a naturalist who, for the first time, has wandered in a Brazilian rain forest . . . the general luxuriance of the vegetation filled me with admiration."

Zoom in for a closer look at Darwin's voyage aboard the *Beagle*.

A tropical rain forest   *Kelp is a habitat for many organisms.*

He also saw examples of interesting adaptations. For example, he wrote, "I could not help noticing how exactly the animals and plants in each region are adapted to each other." A seaweed called kelp fascinated Darwin. Its most striking feature was the large number of species that were associated with it. How do species influence each other because of their interdependence?

Some observations, however, were more puzzling to him and led him to question his previous understanding of the living world. We will return to these observations shortly.

Upon returning to England, Darwin began to think about what he saw. He also expressed a desire to contribute to people's under-

This camouflaged tropical insect resembles a leaf.

standing of the natural world. In a letter to his sister he wrote, "I trust and believe that the time spent in this voyage will produce its full worth in Natural History. And it appears to me that doing what *little* one can do to increase the general stock of knowledge is as respectable an object in life as one in any likelihood can pursue. If I was to throw away [this opportunity] I do think I should never rest quietly in my grave."

During the rest of his life, Darwin would contribute more than "a little" to people's understanding of the natural world. Two years after his return, Darwin hit upon an idea that would revolutionize people's thinking about the living world. His idea was that species change (that is, evolve) across time through a process called descent with modification. This explanation for the origin of diversity, unity, and adaptation would become the foundation of modern biology.

Now that you know what prepared young Darwin for a life of scientific discovery, what about you? What is your life preparing you to do? What would you like to do with the rest of your life? How can you prepare yourself for the life you want? Be ready to discuss these questions.

Darwin's Changing Views

Recall that when Charles Darwin enrolled in Cambridge University at the age of 18, he planned to become a minister. In his autobiography he said, "I did not then in the least doubt the strict and literal truth of every word in the *Bible*." Four years later as he boarded the *Beagle*, he said of himself, "I was quite orthodox [traditional], and I remember being heartily laughed at by several of the officers for quoting the *Bible*."

When Darwin sailed around the world on the *Beagle*, he believed that God had created all living species separately. But shortly after his return to England, he noted in his private diary that his views about the origin of species had begun to change. He started to consider the possibility that new species come instead from previously existing species. He attributed his change in thinking largely to his puzzlement over some observations he made during the voyage. Let's look at two of those observations:

- **Some species in the Galápagos Islands were similar to, but distinct from, species on neighboring islands in the Galápagos. They were also similar to, but distinct from, species found in South America.** When Darwin explored the Galápagos Islands off the coast of Ecuador, he discovered that they were teeming with unique life-forms. He wrote that "the natural history of these islands is eminently curious. . . . Most of the [organisms] are aboriginal [native] creations found no where else; there is even a difference between the inhabitants of the different islands; yet all show a marked relationship with those of America, though separated from that continent by an open space of ocean."

  Darwin noticed that different islands had different types of tortoises. This was true for mockingbirds too. There were also distinct types of finches on each island and plants found nowhere else in the world. Even though distinct types of animals and plants inhabited each island, they were similar to those found on nearby islands and in South America.

Because all scientific ideas depend on observational and experimental confirmation, all scientific knowledge is subject to change as new evidence becomes available.

Similar but distinct mockingbirds inhabit the Galápagos Islands and the mainland of South America. Mockingbirds exist only in the Americas and no place else on Earth.

■ **The fossil remains of extinct animals in South America were similar to, but distinct from, species currently living in South America.** In South America, Darwin found the fossil remains of several types of animals, called glyptodonts, that resemble living armadillos. These animals were not found any place else in the world.

Extinct glyptodonts (left) resemble living armadillos (right).

Darwin was puzzled by groups of similar-looking but distinct species that lived near each other in one part of the world and nowhere else. Why do you think Darwin found these observations puzzling from a natural theology viewpoint?

Recall that natural theology says that each species was created with traits that were just right for surviving and reproducing in the environment it lives in. Therefore, similar-looking species should be found in similar environments. Darwin, however, observed that similar-looking Galápagos mockingbirds inhabited islands that had very different environments. Some of the islands had lush vegetation, while others were mostly desert. Why would similar species have been created for such different environments? And why would so many mockingbird species have been created so close to one another and nowhere else on Earth?

Darwin asked the same questions about the armadillos he saw living in South America. Again, he found similar species living in different environments. Even more puzzling was the resemblance between living armadillos and fossil glyptodonts. The fossil record suggested that armadillo-like animals had lived in South America in the past, gone extinct, and had then been replaced by new armadillo-like species. Why would armadillo-like animals keep appearing in this part of the world and nowhere else?

Because Darwin could not explain these puzzles of nature from a natural theology point of view, he started to consider an alternative explanation. His explanation was that species sometimes split and give rise to new species. The new species retain some similarities with their ancestor, but across time come to look different in some respects from their ancestor and from each other. Darwin called this change in species across time descent with modification. Why do you think Darwin thought he could better explain these observations in terms of new species coming from previously existing species?

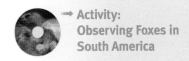

⟹ **Activity:
Observing Foxes in
South America**

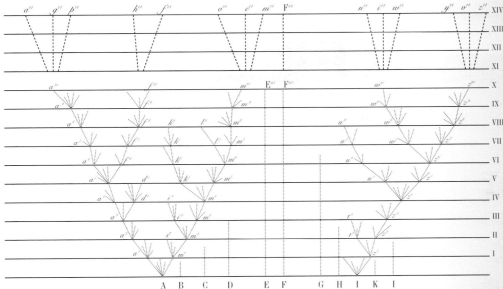

*Depiction of Darwin's drawing of
descent with modification*

If the descent with modification explanation is correct, then you would expect to find similar-looking species living close to one another because the ancestor species that split and gave rise to them had lived in the area. How might this process explain why similar-looking but distinct species of mockingbirds inhabit the various islands of the Galápagos?

Perhaps some mockingbirds from the mainland species were blown out to sea or migrated to one of the Galápagos Islands, reproduced, then changed across time to look somewhat different from, but still similar to, the mainland species. Then maybe some mockingbirds from that island were blown over or migrated to another island where they reproduced and changed across time to look somewhat different from, but still similar to, the other island species and the mainland species. Perhaps this process, occurring over and over again, led to all of the different mockingbird species Darwin saw living near their ancestral mainland species.

Now think about how this process might explain why there are so many similar but distinct species of armadillos living today in

South and Central America and the southern part of North America. Recall that the fossil evidence suggests that an armadillo-like species, like a glyptodont, lived in South America many years ago. What if this species split into several new species that had changed across time? And what if these species had split and changed? Would this process of repeated splitting and changing explain Darwin's observations of living armadillos?

Darwin realized that this idea was speculative and left a lot of things unexplained. For example, how do we know that species *can* change across time? And *how* do they change across time? And, perhaps most important, how do they change across time in such a way that they develop traits that are adaptive for the environments they inhabit? Darwin had to think long and hard before he came up with answers to these questions, and before he could make a case good enough to share with other scientists.

Artificial Selection Provides a Clue to How Species Change

Another observation provided Darwin with an important clue to how species change. All around the English countryside, species were changing across time. In fact, humans were deliberately modifying them through the process of *artificial selection*. For example, dairy cattle had been modified to produce more milk, sheep had been modified to produce higher-quality wool, racehorses had been modified to run faster, crop plants had been modified to produce more edible material, and decorative plants had been modified to produce particular colors of flowers.

The process of modification was the same in each case—selective breeding. For example, a sheep breeder who wanted more wool would carefully select the sheep that would be the parents of the next generation. The breeder would select only those males with the most wool and mate them with females that had the most wool. By doing this, the offspring of the next generation would likely have more wool than if they had been born to parents with less wool. The breeder would then carefully select among the offspring only the best wool-producing sheep to be parents of the next generation. The breeder continued this process for many generations until the sheep were producing much more wool than earlier generations.

Animal and plant breeders showed Darwin that species could change across time and develop useful traits. Through the process of artificial selection, domesticated species developed traits that

➡ **Activity:**
Investigating Variation on Evolutionary Change in Fast Plants

were useful to humans. Darwin wondered if a natural process of modifying species, similar to artificial selection, led wild species to develop traits that were useful for members of the species. He eventually hit on that natural process.

Suppose that members of a species vary with regard to various traits such as size, shape, color, and behavior. As a result, some individuals are better able to survive and reproduce in their environment than others. For example, some individuals might have traits that allow them to compete better for food. Or some individuals might have traits that provide better defenses against predators. These traits might make them more likely to survive and reproduce. Darwin said that organisms having such traits were "fitter." What other differences among individuals of a species might affect their ability to survive and reproduce (that is, their fitness)?

Now suppose that fitness-influencing traits can be inherited. That is, individuals with fitness-*enhancing* traits tend to pass these traits to their offspring. Individuals with fitness-reducing traits also tend to pass these traits to their offspring.

Are these speculations reasonable? If these speculations are correct, Darwin reasoned, then individuals with fitness-enhancing traits would leave more offspring than individuals with fitness-reducing traits, and the offspring would have the fitness-enhancing traits of their parents. This would cause the proportion of individuals with fitness-enhancing traits to increase from one generation to the next. You could say that individuals with the fitness-enhancing traits were "naturally selected" to be the parents of the next generation. As Darwin wrote, "I have called this principle, by which each slight variation, if useful, is preserved, by the term 'Natural Selection.'" You will explore natural selection in more detail in Chapter 5, "Evolution in Action."

Artificial selection can transform the appearance of a species.

Darwin and Religion

Were Darwin's ideas about evolution antireligious? To answer this question, you must consider both Darwin's personal and professional opinions.

Darwin personally felt that his theory of evolution allowed God a place in the creation of species. It was common for scientists in Darwin's time to think that God had designed the general rules or laws that governed the universe, but that God was not directly responsible for the details of every single event that occurred. For example, God had designed gravity and the laws of motion to govern the way objects such as planets and falling rocks moved. God was not, however, directly responsible for the direction and speed at which every object in the universe was moving. God had also designed the laws of reproduction and inheritance.

Darwin suggested that God may have created the general rules or laws that govern the origin of new species, rather than directly creating each species separately. In fact, he began his first book on evolution with a quote from a famous scientist at the time (William Whewell) who wrote, "With regard to the material world, we can at least go so far as this—we can perceive that events are brought about not by insulated interpositions [exercise] of Divine power, exerted in each particular case, but by the establishment of general laws."

Darwin even went so far as to suggest that this was a more dignified view of God. It was more dignified to suppose that God had the wisdom and power to devise general laws that govern the origin and adaptive evolution of species, rather than deal with the details of each species separately.

Darwin was interested in religious issues, and he thought about the religious implications of his theory. After all, he had once considered becoming a minister, although he had not taken that path. He had become a scientist instead. Professionally, however, Darwin preferred to leave discussions about the religious implications of evolution to theologians. He had little to say publicly about these issues. When he did comment, he liked to emphasize that "I am fully aware that I am traveling beyond my proper province." In other words, he was traveling beyond his own province of science into the province of religion.

How Darwin Worked as a Scientist

As you can see, Darwin made new observations about the natural world as he traveled. Afterward he wrote, "It appears to me that nothing can be more improving to a young naturalist, than a journey in distant countries." What did he do with all those observations? He thought hard about them and tried to understand what they meant about the natural world.

An important part of a scientist's work is logical thinking. Scientists think about how their observations fit into people's current understanding of the world. They also think about what their understanding does *not* explain. The way people in a society think about and understand the world influences what a scientist

"What is the hardest task in the world? To think."

Ralph Waldo Emerson,
American poet and philosopher

does and, sometimes, what a scientist thinks. In the next section, you will discover more about how people in Darwin's society thought about the natural world. This is important to know because it shows what an independent and radical thinker Darwin became after he returned home from the *Beagle*.

Darwin's observations during and after his voyage eventually caused him to reject some of his society's cherished ideas about the natural world and to develop a new and different understanding. This understanding became the foundation of modern biology. Let's look at a few more ideas about the natural world that Darwin challenged.

TAKE CHARGE
OF YOUR LEARNING

Think of a recent discovery in science that changed people's understanding of the natural world. How did you learn about this discovery? How do people today learn about new scientific discoveries? Be ready to describe the discovery.

Darwin Interprets the World Differently

Natural theology says that species are perfectly adapted to their environment because they have been designed by God. Yet Darwin noticed many imperfections in nature. Traits like useless pelvic bones in snakes were evidence against perfect design.

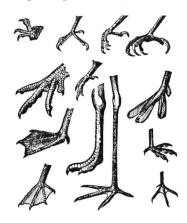

Furthermore, supposedly perfect traits (like the human eye) were not perfect at all. For example, we all have a blind spot where the optic nerve leaves the back of the eyeball. In fact, most organisms looked more like odd contraptions put together by a tinkerer rather than a master designer. Darwin eventually concluded that a natural explanation accounted for the imperfections in nature better than any other explanation. He later used these imperfections as evidence of evolution.

A bird's foot is adapted for a certain lifestyle. For what lifestyle does a webbed foot adapt a bird? What about a foot with long, curved claws? Are these traits perfect? How do you know? Be prepared to present evidence to support your view.

Another idea Darwin challenged was essentialism, or thinking in terms of fixed types. Essentialism sorts things in nature into separate, unchanging types. Each type is defined by its own essence or unique set of ideal and unchanging traits. Scientists commonly looked at species this way during

Some snakes have tiny, useless pelvic bones even though they do not have legs.

No two zebras have the same stripe pattern. They differ slightly in all other traits too.

Individual variation is one of the key elements of Darwin's theory of evolution.

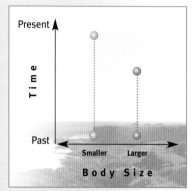

An essentialist view of life. Each species (orange circle and blue circle) has a separate origin and does not change across time. Species can, however, go extinct.

Zoom in for a closer look at variation.

Darwin's time. They thought that species were separate, unrelated, unchanging "natural kinds." In their view, one species could not change into another species. This meant that the variation people saw in zebras, for example, was not important for the future of the species. All zebras were just variations of the ideal zebra.

While other scientists disregarded variation and thought each species was a fixed type, Darwin did not. He eventually came to realize that variation within a species was biologically important because it was the raw material for evolution. Darwin noticed that a species was made up of populations of individuals and that each individual was unique. Some were taller or faster or more colorful than others. Darwin saw these variations as key to a species's future. He became convinced that these differences were important in understanding how evolution occurred. This focus on the variation among individuals within populations and its importance for evolution is called population thinking.

Once Darwin rejected the idea of unchanging types, he was able to think about species changing across time. Once he rejected the idea that species were perfectly adapted to their environment, he was ready to think about how natural processes might produce adaptation.

Within a year of returning from the voyage of the *Beagle* (1837), Darwin's observations convinced him that evolution was occurring. A year later, he proposed a mechanism for evolution—natural selection.

In 1844, eight years after the voyage of the *Beagle*, Darwin summarized his ideas about evolution in a 200-page outline. He did not publish the outline, but shared it with a few close friends. He knew that he would need a lot of evidence to convince people that his ideas were correct. He spent 21 years (from 1837 to 1858) gathering evidence. During this time, he made more observations in the field, read widely, communicated with other scientists and animal breeders, and thought long and hard about evolution.

One of the world's most respected evolutionary biologists, Ernst Mayr, described Darwin's approach as one of "continually going back and forth between making observations, posing questions, establishing hypotheses or models, testing them by making further observations, and so forth." This is the same approach scientists use today.

Darwin knew that his theory would have to explain how the diversity of species, the similarities among species (unity), and adaptation came about through natural processes. Before we look at his explanation in more detail, let's look at how some people before Darwin tried to explain these observations.

Natural Explanations for Diversity, Unity, and Adaptation

Modern science is based on the idea that natural processes account for the natural world. Therefore, scientists try to develop *natural* (or *naturalistic*) *explanations* for what they see. Natural explanations do not use any supernatural events or processes. This is because scientists cannot observe, measure, or experiment with the supernatural. It is outside the realm of science.

An elderly Charles Darwin

Charles Darwin was not the first person to propose a natural explanation for the diversity, unity, and adaptations of life. In fact, more than two dozen naturalists before him proposed such explanations. These explanations date back more than 2,000 years. Many of them, however, are speculation. There is little or no evidence to support them. In contrast, Darwin had evidence to support his explanation. Some of these earlier explanations also make inaccurate predictions, whereas Darwin's made accurate predictions about what scientists should observe about the living world.

Let's look at how some naturalists before Darwin tried to explain the living world. Although most of these explanations have fallen into history's dustbin, a few are still around today. As you read each one, think about whether you know anyone who uses it to explain observations about the living world. Think also about whether you know of any evidence that disproves it or supports it.

Some of the earliest recorded naturalistic explanations for diversity, unity, and adaptation were written by ancient Greek

Scientific explanations must meet certain criteria. They must be consistent with evidence and make accurate predictions. They should also be logical, be open to criticism, report methods and procedures, and be made public.

● **TAKE CHARGE**
OF YOUR LEARNING

As you read, identify what the naturalist was trying to explain—diversity, unity, or adaptation. Record your answers in your notebook. Be ready to explain your reasoning.

philosopher-naturalists. For example, around 580 B.C., Anaximander speculated that "living creatures arose from the moist element as it was evaporated by the sea."

A hundred years later, Empedocles (ca. 500–430 B.C.) speculated that parts of organisms sprang from the earth and combined randomly, sometimes producing monsters. The monsters did not survive, but those with the right number and arrangement of parts did. The survivors were the first members of the many species we see today. Later still, Lucretius (ca. 99–55 B.C.) speculated that whole organisms sprang from the earth. Like Empedocles, he thought some of them were monsters that did not survive. Those that did survive were the first of their species.

Around 1800, the French scientist Lamarck speculated that species evolved across time and proposed a mechanism for evolutionary change. His mechanism was the inheritance of acquired

Lamarck and Darwin had different explanations for how traits such as long legs in birds came about.

traits. Lamarck thought that changing environmental conditions created new needs for organisms. As organisms increased or decreased the use of their body parts to meet those needs, their body parts changed. They passed those changes to their offspring through inheritance. For example, a bird that waded in shallow water might stretch its legs to keep its body out of the water. This stretching would cause the bird's legs to get longer. The bird would then pass that trait to its offspring.

Lamarck also thought that all species tended to evolve toward increasing complexity. Since this would eventually result in only complex organisms being present, he speculated that new microorganisms appeared spontaneously in the environment.

Although Lamarck's ideas seemed reasonable and convincing to many, Darwin rejected them because there was not much evidence to support them. In fact, scientists later conducted experiments showing that the inheritance of acquired traits was not correct. In one experiment, they cut off the tails of mice for many generations and discovered that newborn mice were always born with tails. Other observations demonstrated that species were not evolving toward increasing complexity and that microorganisms were not spontaneously appearing in the modern environment.

Of all the thinkers before Darwin, Patrick Matthew (1831) came the closest to developing an explanation like Darwin's. In fact, Darwin wrote that Matthew "most expressly and clearly anticipated my views."

Like Darwin, Matthew could not always tell the difference between a variety and a species. He also realized that if humans could produce new varieties of animals in just a few short years through the practice of artificial selection (selective breeding), then maybe nature could produce new species over the long course of Earth's history.

Unfortunately for Matthew, his ideas went unnoticed until after Darwin published *On the Origin of Species*. This was because Matthew published his description of "diverging ramification" (evolution) and natural selection in the appendix of a little-read book about shipbuilding and growing trees for ship construction. Furthermore, he did *not* support his ideas with evidence the way Darwin did. Nor did he appreciate or work out its implications the way Darwin did.

About natural selection, Matthew wrote, "To me the conception of this law of nature came intuitively as a self-evident fact. . . . He [Darwin] seems to have worked it out by inductive reason [putting facts together and drawing conclusions], slowly and with due cau-tion to have made his way synthetically from fact to fact onwards; while with me it was by a general glance at the scheme of nature that I estimated select production of species as a recognizable fact—requiring only to be pointed out to be admitted by unprejudiced minds with sufficient grasp."

Although Matthew thought the operation of natural selection would be obvious to people once he pointed it out, it was not. Darwin's description of natural selection gained wide acceptance among scientists because he provided evidence and explained its significance. Rather than assuming that natural selection would be obvious to people, Darwin collected facts and used logical reasoning to show people that it was the mechanism of evolution-ary change.

Despite the writings of these and other naturalists down through history, only Lamarck and Erasmus Darwin (Charles's grandfather) were known for their evolutionary views when Darwin started his first notebook on evolution in 1837. Nearly all other scientists at

All varieties of pigeons are descendants of the rock pigeon. Humans produced these varieties through selective breeding.

Alfred Russel Wallace

In communicating and defending the results of scientific inquiry, arguments must be logical and demonstrate connections among observations, investigations, and historical knowledge.

After reading about Darwin's theory in *On the Origin of Species*, naturalist Thomas Henry Huxley said, "How extremely stupid not to have thought of that myself." He became a vocal defender of Darwin's ideas and got the nickname "Darwin's bulldog."

the time thought that species had been specially created. Remember, even Darwin believed this when he traveled around the world on the *Beagle*.

In 1858, a scientist named Alfred Russel Wallace independently developed the same explanation as Darwin for diversity, unity, and adaptation. He sent it to Darwin to read, and later that year, two of Darwin's colleagues read Darwin's and Wallace's scientific papers on evolution by natural selection at a meeting of the Linnaean Society in England. Surprisingly, none of the scientists at the meeting realized the significance of their ideas. In fact, the president of the society later described the year as lacking "any of those striking discoveries which at once revolutionize" science. He was wrong. A century later, biologist Theodosius Dobzhansky said, "Nothing in biology makes sense except in the light of evolution."

Despite the cool reception his ideas received at the Linnaean Society meeting, Darwin spent the next year getting his book ready for publication while interest in it grew. All 1,250 copies of *On the Origin of Species* sold out in one day. The book sparked a passionate debate about the workings of nature and the origin of species, especially humans. Most scientists, however, accepted Darwin's ideas because his evidence and reasoning were persuasive.

The idea that species evolve (change across time) and are related to each other through descent from common ancestors came to be accepted by most scientists within Darwin's lifetime. His proposal that natural selection was an important reason for evolutionary change was not fully accepted until the early 1900s. Natural selection is one of several forces of evolutionary change. You'll read about the others in Chapter 4, "The Genetic Basis of Evolution."

Five Key Ideas of Darwin's Theory of Biological Evolution

Darwin's theory of evolution consists of five key ideas. Before Darwin, no one had put these ideas together with the evidence to support them. Darwin's genius was to bring them all together into one well-supported theory. The five ideas are the following:

1. Species evolve. The traits of all species change across time. A species is composed of populations of individuals who can mate and produce offspring. Individuals do not evolve. Only groups of individuals of the same species (populations) evolve.

2. Species evolve from common ancestors. Species that evolve from the same ancestor species are related. Ultimately, all groups of organisms, including animals, plants, fungi, and microorganisms, can trace their history back to the same ancestor. Common descent explains the many similarities among organisms.

3. New species form from existing species (speciation). For example, a new species often forms when a group of individuals becomes geographically isolated from other members of its species. The group evolves or changes into a new species as natural selection adapts it to its new surroundings. Other mechanisms of speciation also are important, especially in plants.

4. Evolution usually occurs gradually. Darwin emphasized that evolutionary change usually takes place slowly across millions of years, but he did not rule out the possibility of more rapid change.

5. Natural selection is the most important mechanism by which adaptive evolution occurs. Natural selection is a process in which individuals who are better adapted to the environment tend to produce more offspring than individuals who are less well adapted. This causes the traits of a group to change across time. Natural selection results in the members of a group becoming, on average, better adapted to the environment.

These five ideas made Darwin a rebel scientist in his day. Why? Because he challenged some of his society's most cherished beliefs. Although many people considered Darwin a rebel when he published his book, *On the Origin of Species,* in 1859, his natural explanation for species diversity, species similarities, and adaptation became the foundation for the modern theory of evolution. Today, evolution is one of the organizing principles in biology. ●

➡ **Activity:**
Past and Present
Explanations for Diversity,
Unity, and Adaptation

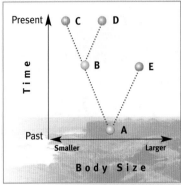

Evolutionary view of life. Species B, C, D, and E all evolved from species A. Therefore, species A is their ancient ancestor. Species B is a recent common ancestor of D and C. Notice that the body size of all species has changed across time. Other traits change too. Species can go extinct (E).

The millions of different plants, animals, and microorganisms that live on Earth today are related by descent from common ancestors.

Evidence of Evolution

Chapter 3

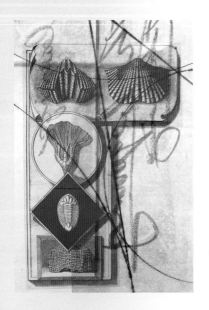

L
ook at the drawing on this page. What biological idea do you think the artist is trying to communicate? What would convince you that this idea is correct? Write your answers in your notebook and then continue reading. You'll get another chance to interpret the meaning of this drawing at the end of the chapter.

Science Is Based on Evidence

In Chapter 1, you discovered that science is a way of knowing. How is science similar to and different from other ways of knowing, such as art?

Recall that the natural sciences try to explain the natural world through natural processes. For example, natural scientists want to know what natural process produced the world's estimated 13 million or more species. What natural process explains the structural and molecular similarities among different species? What natural process adapts species to their environments?

One of the most important characteristics of scientific knowledge is that it is based on *evidence*. This means that the scientific explanation for the diversity and similarities among species, as well as how they became suited to their environment, must be supported by evidence from observations and experiments.

Keep in mind that all scientific explanations for the natural world must meet the following criteria:

- They must be supported by information (data) collected through observations and experiments.

- They must make predictions that can be verified by additional observations and experiments.

- They must be logical. This means they cannot contain contradictory ideas.

- They must be communicated to the scientific community and the public and be open to critical review.

- They must be changed if new evidence shows that they are incomplete or incorrect.

- They must account for the world through the operation of natural processes.

TAKE CHARGE
OF YOUR LEARNING

As you read through the rest of the chapter, keep track of one example for each pillar of evidence.

Evolution Is a Powerful Explanation for Diversity, Unity, and Adaptations of Life

In 1858, Charles Darwin and Alfred Russel Wallace proposed that life was evolving and that the mechanism of adaptive evolutionary change was natural selection. Generations of scientists who followed them have refined and expanded their explanation for life's diversity, unity, and adaptations. Today, most scientists find the evidence of biological evolution so overwhelming that they consider its occurrence as a fundamental principle.

What is the evidence that evolution has occurred in the past and is still occurring today? Seven pillars of evidence support the idea that life evolves. Darwin talked about five of them. The last two were not discovered until after Darwin's death, primarily because scientists needed modern technology to collect the data. Let's examine the evidence in more detail.

What Is the Evidence of Evolution?

The seven pillars of evidence of evolution are (**1**) the fossil record, (**2**) the structural similarities among organisms, (**3**) the geographic distribution of organisms, (**4**) the embryological similarities among organisms, (**5**) the pattern of organism groupings, (**6**) the molecular similarities among organisms, and (**7**) direct observation of evolutionary changes in the laboratory and in the wild.

Pillar of Evidence 1: The Fossil Record

Recall from Chapter 2 that the discovery of more and more fossils caused Darwin and several other naturalists to challenge the idea of unchanging species. If nature did not change, why did fossils make it appear that some species had changed across time or had died out?

An early explanation was that fossils were just jokes of nature—rocks that accidentally resembled living things. By the early 1800s, however, the fossil data convinced most scientists that fossils were not jokes of nature, but the preserved remains of species that no longer existed.

Scientists also knew that Earth is made up of different layers of rock and that each layer contains distinctive fossils. Darwin was one of the first scientists to realize that the fossil record was evidence that species evolve across time. In fact, he devoted an entire chapter in his book *On the Origin of Species* to the fossil record.

Evolution by natural selection explains the diversity, the unity, and the adaptations of life better than any other naturalistic explanation.

The fossil record provides information about the rates of evolution and history of life.

Rocks and Fossils

Fossils provide scientists with information about the history of life on Earth. A *fossil* is any preserved part or impression of an organism that lived in the past.

Scientists find fossils all around the world, mostly in *sedimentary* rocks. Sedimentary rocks form when sediments such as sand or clay are compressed by overlying sediments and change to stone. If the sediment contains the remains of an organism, sometimes the remains change to stone too (fossilize). Common sedimentary rocks are sandstone and limestone.

Water and wind lay down sedimentary rocks in layers. These layers sometimes contain fossils.

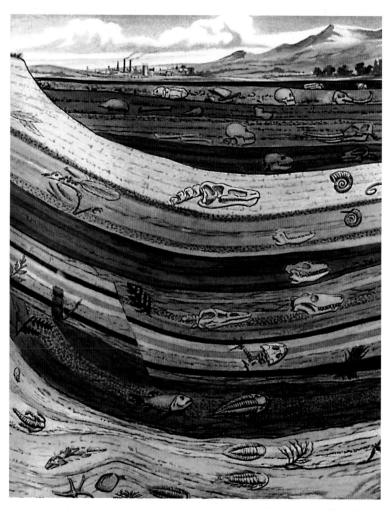

Sedimentary rocks occur in layers called strata. Scientists can identify each layer by the type of sediment that changed into rock. The strata are arranged with the youngest at the top and the oldest on the bottom. So when you dig into the Earth, it's like taking a trip into the past. The sequence of the fossil record in the rocks tells the story of Earth's history from the present to the past, including the history of species.

Darwin recognized that fossils did not form very often. Most of the time, dead organisms decay or are eaten. But sometimes, all or some of their body parts fossilize. Usually, the hard parts of organisms (such as bones, teeth, or shells) fossilize, not the soft parts (such as meat and fat). This is because the hard parts decay slowly, whereas the soft parts decay quickly. For this reason, many fossils that survive are those of complex animals. Impressions such as footprints, feather prints, and leaf prints can fossilize too.

Fossils form in several ways. Some fossils form when minerals dissolved in groundwater seep into the tissues of a dead organism and turn it to stone. This is called petrification. Others form when organisms get buried in the mud at the bottom of lakes and rivers. As the organisms decay, minerals in the water replace the body tissues and form a cast in the shape of the organisms. Occasionally, the impressions organisms make in mud or sand dry and turn to stone. These impressions are called imprints.

Some fossils form when organisms get trapped and preserved in amber or tar. Amber is a sticky substance produced by evergreen trees that hardens when it dries. Tar is a gooey, oily substance that sometimes forms in the ground when plant material decays. Finally, fossils sometimes form when organisms are covered by snow or ice and freeze before they start to decay.

The Fossil Record Reveals Evolution

Recall that evolution is descent with modification (descent from common ancestors with change over time). Darwin was one of the first to use the concept. For example, the theory of evolution predicts that ancestors and their descendants will usually (but not always) be different. The fossil record shows that some fossil species are similar in form to living ones, but most are very different. This observation suggests that most species have changed across long stretches of time.

Because the fossils found in Earth's rocks provide information about organisms that lived in the past, scientists can use the fossil record to test (that is, to support or refute) the idea that life evolves. The theory of evolution predicts that most species that lived in the distant past should be very different from the species that exist today. The fossil record supports this prediction. The vast majority of fossil species are different from the species living today.

Because the characteristics of most species are changing slowly across time, descendants tend to look increasingly different from their ancestors. Such change is well documented in a wide variety of plant and animal species because the environment in the distant past was very different from the environment today.

Evolution also predicts that where fossils appear in the strata will be consistent with the idea of descent with modification. The fossil record supports this prediction. Fishes, amphibians, reptiles, primitive mammals, and modern mammals appear sequentially in the fossil record; they are not mixed together at random.

For instance, about 1.2 billion years ago the first animal appears in the fossil record. At the beginning of the Cambrian period nearly 600 million years ago, invertebrate animals are abundant. Nearly 100 million years later, the first fishes appear. Still another hundred million or so years pass before the first amphibians appear. Another hundred million years pass before the first reptiles, and still another hundred million pass before the first mammals. A pattern of appearance is observed for plant fossils too. Algae, for example, first appear more than 3 billion years ago and flowering plants around 150 million years ago.

Evolution also predicts that younger rocks will contain more fossils that resemble living species than older rocks. The fossil record supports this prediction. One study made during Darwin's time showed that 96 percent of fossil shell species found in rocks that are 1.8–5 million years old belonged to species that were still in existence. However, only 3 percent of the fossil species found in rocks that are 34–55 million years old still exist.

Another prediction of evolution is that younger rocks will contain fossils of more complex organisms than older rocks. The fossil record supports this prediction too. The oldest fossil-containing rocks on Earth are about 3.5 billion years old. These rocks contain only fossils of simple bacteria (prokaryotes). Around 2 billion years ago, more complex single-celled eukaryotes appear. By 500 million years ago, fossils of still more complex multicellular animals and plants begin to appear. By 70 million years ago, a large variety of very complex fossil organisms are present, including dinosaurs.

Evolution predicts that most species change across time, but it doesn't require that this happen. For example, one scientist has documented a gradual size increase in an ocean-living, shelled protozoan called Pseudocubus across 2 million years. The horseshoe crab, on the other hand, has changed little during hundreds of millions of years. If a species's environment (such as the deep ocean) remains

Zoom in on how scientists measure the age of rocks and fossils.

stable for long periods of time, little change may occur. Most species, however, have lived in changing environments, which explains why most fossils appear different from living species.

Successive changes in the fossil record indicate an *evolutionary trend*. An evolutionary trend is a long-term directional change. The fossil record shows evolutionary trends for many groups of animals and plants. Some trends show increasing complexity, other trends show decreasing complexity.

One of the most complete and best-studied fossil records is that of horses, which dates back about 55 million years. It shows successive changes in several body parts, including the feet, head, and teeth. The trends in horse evolution show directional changes in skull shape and size, brain size and complexity, tooth structure, leg and tail length, and body size. These changes, however, did not take place at a constant rate, and reversals sometimes occurred.

Horseshoe crabs have remained relatively unchanged for the past 250 million years.

Skull size in horses increased from approximately 13 centimeters (5 inches) to nearly 61 centimeters (2 feet) during the past 55 million years. Body size increased from 50 centimeters (20 inches) tall to 155 centimeters (60 inches) tall.

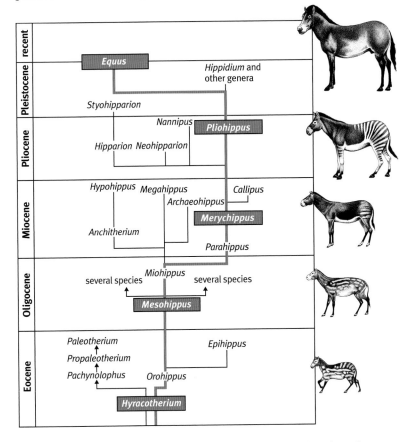

Paleontologists (scientists who study fossils) have fossil evidence that the modern horse (which is classified in the genus *Equus*) is the living descendant of a small, ancient horse called *Hyracotherium*. In between them, about two dozen species evolved. During the evolutionary progression from *Hyracotherium* to *Equus*, body size

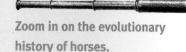

Zoom in on the evolutionary history of horses.

increased, the number of toes on the foot decreased from four to one, and the diet changed from broad-leafed plants to grass.

In fact, the evolutionary tree for horses looks like a bush with many evolutionary branches. The branches represent various horse species that evolved across time. All but one of the branches became extinct. The modern horse is the tip of the only branch to survive to the present day.

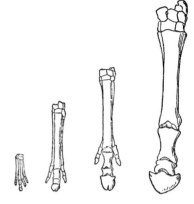

The number of toes in horses has decreased across time from four to one.

Finally, evolution predicts that there should be intermediate, or transitional, fossils that connect groups of organisms such as reptiles and birds, and reptiles and mammals. The fossil record supports this prediction. Scientists recently discovered *Pederpes*, a 350-million-year-old crocodile-like creature that is a stepping-stone between fish and the first four-legged land animals. Archaeopteryx and several recently discovered feathered dinosaurs in China have traits of birds (for example, feathers) and reptiles (a bony tail and teeth). Early mammal-like reptiles (called therapsids) blur the line between reptiles and mammals so much that they are difficult to classify.

TAKE CHARGE
OF YOUR LEARNING

Zoom in on whale evolution. Log on to the Internet and watch an animation of whale evolution at:

http://www.pbs.org/wgbh/ evolution/library/03/4/l_034_05.html.

Recently discovered fossils show how whales evolved during the past 50 million years. The change from a four-limbed land animal to a two-limbed whale is now well documented by transitional forms in the fossil record, strong evidence of evolution.

Like all evidence, the fossil record has limitations. For

Archaeopteryx had feathers like a bird and a bony tail like a reptile.

example, the fossil record is incomplete. It is incomplete because not all parts of organisms fossilize easily. Furthermore, fossilization is a rare event because it requires very specific environmental conditions. Darwin was aware of these limitations and addressed them in his book *On the Origin of Species*. Nonetheless, the fossil evidence known in Darwin's time was sufficient to support his new hypothesis of biological evolution. Today, the fossil record is much better

Activity:
From Landlubber to Leviathan: Exploring the Origin of Whales

known and even more strongly supports the idea that life evolves.
Fossil displays in museums help communicate this evidence to
the public.

Pillar of Evidence 2: Structural Similarities among Organisms

Structural similarities among organisms seen in fossil and living
species provide the second pillar of evidence for evolution. For
example, fish, amphibians, reptiles, birds, and mammals have the
same pattern of bones in their limbs. All insects have three pairs of
legs; flowers show similarities in arrangement of bud leaves, petals,
and sex organs.

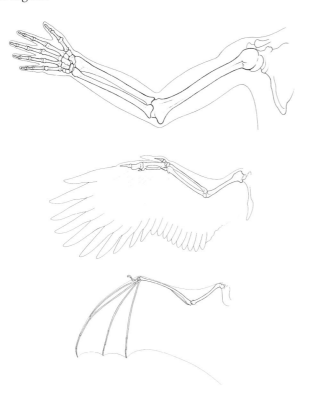

*Humans (top), birds (center), and bats
(bottom) have the same pattern of bones
in their arms.*

Similarities among Bones Reveal Evolution

Darwin pointed out that similar body structures often serve
different functions. Humans, bats, and birds have the same pattern
of bones, but the bones are modified in size and shape for different
functions. Darwin wrote, "We have no reason to believe that the
same bones in the hand of a man, wing of a bat, and fin of a por-
poise, are related to similar conditions of life." To understand what
he meant, complete the Take Charge of Your Learning task.

According to the evolutionary concept of common descent, the ancient common ancestor of all vertebrates (animals with backbones) had the basic pattern of limb bones seen in all vertebrates today. These vertebrates include fish, amphibians, reptiles, birds, and mammals. All of these animals inherited this bone pattern from that ancient common ancestor. Likewise, all insects inherited their leg pattern from their common insect ancestor. And all flowering plants inherited their flower structure from the same flowering ancestor.

Today, when different organisms have similar body structures that suggest descent from a common ancestor, scientists refer to the structures as homologous. Scientists have discovered many types of homologous structures, including body parts and molecules.

Evolution Modifies Common Patterns

As you have just seen, common ancestry explains some structural similarities among organisms. But how, for example, did the homologous bones in the vertebrate limb come to differ in size, shape, and function in different organisms?

To answer this question, Darwin proposed natural selection. He wrote, "The explanation is . . . the natural selection of successive slight modifications—each modification being profitable in some way." In other words, structures inherited from the common ancestor were gradually modified as each vertebrate group became adapted to its environment through the process of natural selection.

Bats, for example, evolved relatively longer finger bones because individuals with longer finger bones had higher fitness than individuals with shorter bones. Longer finger bones function better as scaffolding for the skin that forms the bat's wing. Shorter finger bones evolved in humans. Shorter finger bones are better adapted for grasping and manipulating objects. These are examples of what Darwin called descent with modification from common ancestors. This phrase is a good description of the theory of evolution through natural selection.

Rudimentary Structures Reveal Evolution

Descent with modification also explains the existence of rudimentary (or practically useless) structures. Almost all species have structures that are incompletely formed and serve no useful function today. Humans have an appendix, four shortened and fused tailbones, and reduced muscles that are homologous to muscles in other animals that move the ears. Scientists call such

Long arm and finger bones support the skin that forms the bat's wing.

nonfunctional structures vestigial. Modern research shows
that vestigial structures in other
organisms include nonfunctional eyes in cave-dwelling fish,
pelvic bones in legless whales,
and nonfunctional flowers in
dandelion plants.

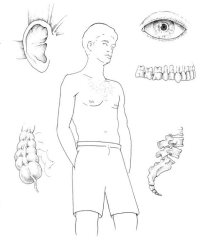

*Vestigial structures in humans include
muscles that wiggle the ears, a nonmov-
able membrane in the corner of the eye,
shortened tailbones, an appendix, and
wisdom teeth that fail to develop.*

Darwin concluded that vestigial structures are remnants left
over from a common ancestor in
whom the structures were fully
formed and functional. Accord-
ing to Darwin, "Such organs are solely due to inheritance . . . and
plainly bespeak of an ancestor having the organ in a useful condi-
tion." Because the descendants of a common ancestor sometimes
encounter different environments and adopt new lifestyles, a structure may no longer be useful. Therefore, natural selection no longer
operates in ways that maintain the structure, and over many generations it becomes nonfunctional.

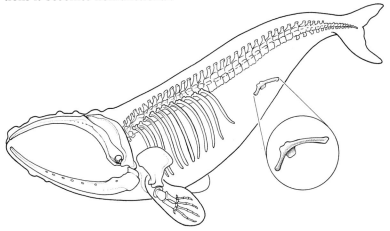

Vestigial pelvic bones (circled) in a whale

Modern research shows that vestigial structures also occur at the
molecular level. For example, all eukaryotic organisms contain
nonfunctional sequences of DNA called a *pseudogenes*. These
genetically silent sequences of DNA are vestiges of once-functional
genes inherited from ancient ancestors.

One such pseudogene explains why all mammals, except
humans and guinea pigs, can synthesize vitamin C. Mammals
inherited a functional version of the gene for synthesizing vitamin
C from an early ancestor. But in humans and guinea pigs, the gene,

Ostrich, 240 centimeters (94 inches) tall

Emu, 180 centimeters (70 inches) tall

Rhea, 152 centimeters (59 inches) tall

Kiwi, 35 centimeters (14 inches) tall

even though present, later mutated and became nonfunctional. As a result, humans and guinea pigs have to obtain vitamin C from their food.

Pillar 2 demonstrates that certain species have similar structures and that these similarities are evidence of evolution from a common ancestor. So how do we account for the differences among species?

Pillar of Evidence 3: The Geographic Distribution of Organisms

Examine the pictures of four birds: an ostrich, an emu, a rhea, and a kiwi. What are their similarities and differences? What additional information do you need?

Notice that all of these birds have feathers. They also have less obvious features in common such as the shape of their breastbone (keel) and the structure of their mouth. You cannot tell from the photos, but they also are all flightless.

Despite these similarities, the birds are in some ways different. For example, they live in different parts of the world. They also differ in size. The ostrich, the largest living bird, reaches a height of almost 240 centimeters (8 feet). The kiwi, on the other hand, is only about 35 centimeters (1 foot) tall.

Did the similarities in their bones, mouths, and inability to fly arise independently in these birds, or do they suggest that these birds had a common ancestor?

We can get clues to answer this question from an area of study called biogeography. Scientists called biogeographers study where species live on Earth, why they live in certain places, how they got there, how they are adapted to their environment, how they are genetically related, and who their ancestors are.

Biogeography provides evidence for evolution, in part, because patterns of distribution today and in the past reflect the origins of related species. Biogeographers think that the ostrich, the kiwi, the rhea, and the emu descended from a common ancestor. The evidence for this is the similarities we noted in their bones and mouths, as well as their forelimbs. They have the same breastbone, the same mouth structure, and they cannot fly. Furthermore, their breastbones, mouths, and forelimbs are different from those in other birds. But that's not all. Their DNA is similar, which suggests that they are closely related.

As you see from the map, these four bird species live in different parts of the world. If they share a common ancestor, how did they

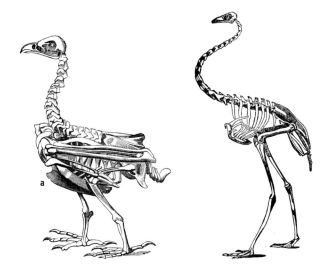

*The breastbone of flying birds (left) has a different structure than the breastbone of flightless birds (right). Powerful flight muscles attach to the breastbone (**a**) in flying birds.*

get to these parts of the world? Did their ancestors walk, or swim, or perhaps fly? How likely are any of these possibilities?

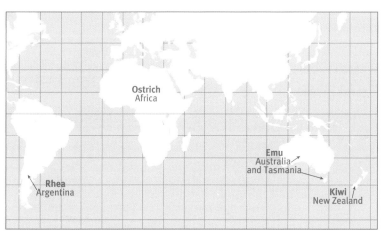

Ostriches, rheas, emus, and kiwis live in different parts of the world.

Darwin wondered the same thing and speculated that the similarities were due to common descent. But he couldn't explain how these birds got to their current locations. It wasn't until the early 1900s that scientists could explain how species found in distant parts of the world could be related to each other through a common ancestor.

Descent with modification from a shared ancestor explains the resemblance between geographically separated species.

Biogeography and Continental Drift

Did you ever notice that the east coast of South America looks like it could fit together with the west coast of Africa? A German scientist named Alfred Wegener noticed this too. In 1915, he proposed the idea of continental drift. He proposed that Earth's landmasses have moved around during Earth's history. Slowly,

Continental drift explains why the coastlines of South America and Africa look like they fit together.

Movements of Earth's landmasses during the past 225 million years (top to bottom)

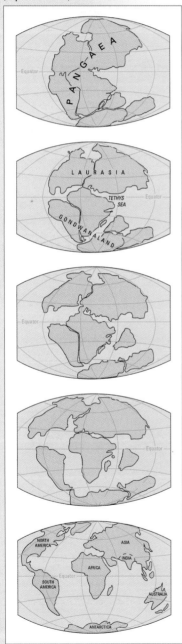

across millions of years, Earth's landmasses have broken apart and shifted to form the continents we recognize today. For example, South America and Africa were once part of a large landmass, but

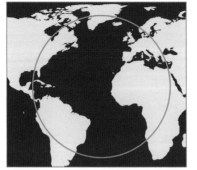

this landmass broke apart and the resulting continents moved to their current locations.

The idea of continental drift is widely accepted by scientists today because it is supported by evidence. Measurements show that Earth's landmasses are moving a few centimeters per year. Geological and biogeographical data provide additional support for continental drift. For example, the same rock formations occur on the west coast of Africa and east coast of Brazil. The discovery of an ancient fossil reptile called Lystrosaurus in South Africa, India, and Antarctica suggests that these lands were once part of a single landmass.

These and other observations led scientists to refine and expand Wegener's idea into the theory of plate tectonics. This theory says that Earth's crust is made up of plates that are composed of continents and ocean floor. These plates move when magma from inside Earth rises to the surface in certain places and forms new crust. As new crust forms, it pushes the existing plates apart. Plate tectonics meets all the criteria of a scientific theory and is one of the foundations of modern earth science.

Are Earth's landmasses still moving? Yes. Earthquakes are more evidence of this. Earthquakes are caused by the tectonic plates moving against each other. In fact, scientists predict that the movements going on today will cause the continents to form into a giant landmass in the next 250 million years.

The theory of plate tectonics helped scientists figure out how flightless birds got to different parts of the world. The geological and biological evidence indicates that about 200 million years ago, Earth's continents formed a giant landmass. Living in many parts of this landmass was an ancient species that was the common ancestor of flightless birds. As the continents slowly broke apart and drifted across the surface of Earth, populations of this ancient bird became isolated. Over millions of years, these isolated populations of birds became increasingly more distinct from each other and their ancient common ancestor as natural selection adapted them to their different environments. Slowly the ostrich, emu, rhea, and kiwi evolved, but they retained traits that show they are descended from a common ancestor.

Zoom in. Log on the Internet and go to the PALEOMAP Project Web site: *http://www.scotese.com /pangeanim.htm* **to watch an animation of continental drift.**

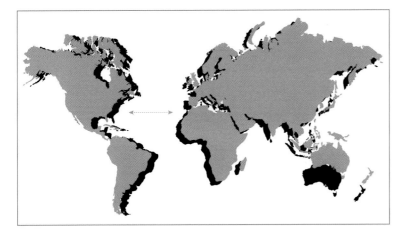

Predicted movements of Earth's continents during the next 250 million years. (The black areas show the location of the continents today. The color areas show their locations 250 million years from now.)

Biogeography as Evidence for Evolution

As Darwin traveled across South America, he noticed differences and similarities among neighboring populations of animals, such as armadillos and rheas. Distinct types inhabited different areas, but they were remarkably similar to their neighbors. What was the explanation for this? Darwin eventually realized that the differences he saw were due to geographical separation followed by modification through natural selection. The similarities were due to common descent.

As the ancestors of these animals spread out across the continent, their separated populations gradually evolved differences. In some cases, they had changed so much that individuals from different populations would not interbreed. The populations had evolved into different species. But they were similar, too, because they evolved from the same ancestor and had inherited many of their ancestor's traits.

➟ Activity: Evolving around the world

When Darwin visited the Cape Verde Islands off the coast of Africa and the Galápagos Islands off the coast of South America, he noticed that the birds found on these islands closely resembled those found on the closest mainland. The birds on Cape Verde resembled species found in Africa, whereas the birds on the Galápagos resembled those found in South America. After his voyage, Darwin realized that descent with modification from common ancestors explained these observations. Some birds from the mainlands had flown or been blown to the islands. These birds started a new, isolated population that evolved across time

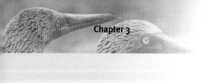

into a different species as natural selection adapted them to their new island environment.

Biogeography provides evidence for evolution (that is, descent with modification from common ancestors). Darwin dedicated a whole chapter in *On the Origin of Species* to this pillar of evidence.

Zoom in on Darwin's discoveries in South America and the Galápagos Islands.

Pillar of Evidence 4: Embryological Similarities among Organisms

Scientists have observed structural, developmental, and molecular similarities among embryos. In *On the Origin of Species*, Darwin provided several examples of similarities among embryos as evidence of evolution. Descent with modification from common ancestors explains these similarities.

Modern research in developmental biology has provided new data that support Darwin's ideas. Scientists have discovered that *all* animals with left and right sides to their bodies (bilateral animals), including worms, flies, and humans, share features of development. These *developmental homologies* include the formation of (**1**) back and belly sides of the body, (**2**) a head and tail region, (**3**) body segments, (**4**) a central nervous system that is divided into different functional regions, (**5**) a gut for digesting food, (**6**) a heartlike pump, (**7**) light-sensing organs, and (**8**) appendages (such as limbs).

In addition, a relatively small number of *developmental genes* control the formation of this shared body plan. These genes occur in all bilateral animals, have similar DNA sequences, and play similar developmental roles. For example, *Pax* developmental genes control the early formation of eyes, whereas *tinman* genes control the formation of heartlike structures.

Descent from common ancestors explains developmental similarities among organisms.

The shared set of developmental genes in animals implies that all animals descended from a common ancestor that had these genes. This ancient ancestor lived more than 550 million years ago. Through the process of natural selection, the later stages of development in various animal groups were modified, producing the enormous diversity of body structures we see among animals today.

Other signs of common ancestry include the temporary appearance of structures during development. For example, the embryos of toothless whales form toothbuds that disappear before development is complete. The larvae of some land frogs develop gills, then lose them. The embryos of cows and sheep temporarily develop chisel-like front teeth (incisors) in their upper jaws, which never emerge.

Why do embryos form such incomplete structures? The most likely natural explanation is descent with modification. In other words, these unused (vestigial) structures remain part of a genetically determined plan of development that was inherited from ancestors in whom the structures were fully developed and useful.

The resemblance among embryos of different species provides still more evidence of descent from common ancestors. Even in the 1800s, naturalists knew that the embryos of different species resembled each other much more closely than do the adults. The embryos of fish, amphibians, reptiles, birds, and mammals look similar early in development. But as development proceeds, they look more and more different.

Embryos of 13 animals at three stages of development (early, intermediate, and late). The embryos more closely resemble each other earlier in development, especially for groups of animals such as mammals (the cat, bat, and human) and fishes (the dogfish, gar, salmon, and lungfish).

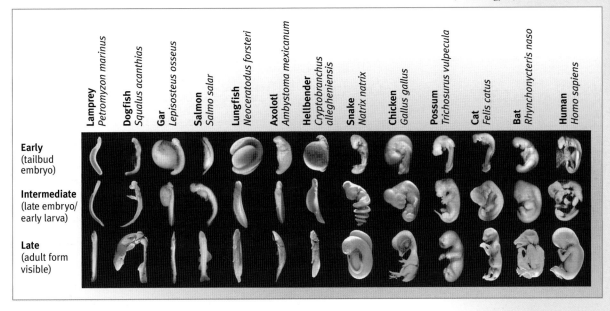

Embryologist Karl von Baer proposed a rule that accounted for this observation. He said that general body features appear in the embryo *before* specialized features. As a result, the embryonic development of a species resembles the embryonic development of its evolutionary ancestors. This is what you would expect by descent with modification from common ancestors.

To see what von Baer meant, let's look at the *branchial arch*. The embryos of all animals that have backbones pass through an early stage of development in which slitlike branchial arches form in the neck region. In fishes and some amphibians, these arches develop into gills. In reptiles, birds, and mammals, they develop into other specialized features such as bones of the skull or middle ear, or into nerves. These arches are part of the same general plan of development that all animals with backbones inherited from their ancient common ancestor. The different structures that the arches change into in different animal groups are examples of evolutionary modification.

It is important to remember that embryos *do not* repeat the *adult* stages of their evolutionary ancestors. For example, the human embryo never looks like an adult fish or forms gills. But it does resemble a fish embryo early in development because both form branchial arches.

During the history of life, the various branches on the tree of life passed their basic plan of development—with small but important changes—to new branches that sprouted from them. This common plan of development and the changes in different evolutionary branches are evidence for descent with modification from common ancestors.

Pillar of Evidence 5: The Pattern of Organism Groupings

As you have seen, the similarities among organisms are evidence of their descent from a common ancestor. These similarities also form the basis of biological classification, or taxonomy. Scientists place organisms with similar body structures, embryological development, and molecules into the same groups. These taxonomic groups described by humans are a way to organize information, but the patterns on which they are based provide evidence of descent from common (shared) ancestors.

Early naturalists noticed that species can be clustered naturally into a hierarchical pattern of groups within groups—that is, species into genera, genera into families, families into orders, and so on. But it was not obvious why these natural groups occur.

It was Darwin who realized that "this natural subordination of organic beings into groups under groups" could be explained by descent with modification from common (shared) ancestors. There is no logical reason to expect species to be arranged hierarchically if they arise separately.

Although scientists today may interpret taxonomic data differently and produce slightly different classification schemes, they agree with the idea of descent with modification from common ancestors. Descent with modification explains two features that are characteristic of organism groupings. First, the pattern is *hierarchical*, or made of groups within groups. Second, it is *branching* or treelike.

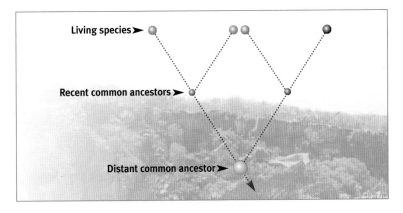

Branching evolutionary history due to descent with modification from common ancestors. Closely related species are grouped into genera, genera into families, and so on.

A branching pattern of groups results whenever an ancestral group splits into related subgroups that come to differ in some way. This pattern allows the ancestry of the subgroups to be traced back to their common ancestor. The ancestry of this ancestor can be traced back to another shared ancestor, and so on.

It's like working backward along the branches of a tree from the twigs to the trunk. You can trace the growth of all twigs back through a series of branch points to the trunk. The twigs represent existing species, nearby branch points represent recent shared ancestors, and the trunk represents a distant ancestor that is common to many branches.

Descent with modification also explains the hierarchical pattern of classification. Recall that a hierarchy contains several levels, such as the species level and the genus level. Each level is nested within a larger level and contains one or more groups of organisms. For example, several species are within the genus level. All of the organisms in a particular group are more similar to each other than they are to organisms in other groups.

For example, lions, tigers, and leopards are three groups of animals. Because lions only mate and produce offspring with other lions in nature, biologists classify them as a species. The same is true for tigers and leopards. Lions, tigers, and leopards represent

Lions (Panthera leo) [left], tigers (Panthera tigris) [middle], and leopards (Panthera pardus) [right] are three species of "big cats."

three taxa (that is, named groups of organisms: *leo*, *tigris*, and *pardus*) at the species level of the classification hierarchy.

Although lions, tigers, and leopards do not interbreed, they do have many traits in common. They have enough traits in common that biologists classify them as different species within the same genus (*Panthera*). The genus is the next level in the hierarchy and contains the species level. *Panthera* and other genera, such as the wildcat (*Felis silvestris*), have enough traits in common that biologists put them together in the same family, Felidae (the cat family). The family is the next level in the hierarchy.

This classification shows the relatedness of species because all members of a taxonomic group—from species to phylum—share a common ancestor. For example, all mammals (class Mammalia), share a remote ancestor. Dogs, cats, and bears (order Carnivora) share a more recent ancestor, and the various cats (family Felidae) share a more recent ancestor still.

Like all the other lines of evidence presented so far, the branching, hierarchical pattern of taxonomic groups supports the idea that evolution involves descent with modification from common ancestors.

Additional Taxonomic Levels

Felidae		
Panthera		**Felis**
leo	tigris pardus	silvestris

Partial taxonomic hierarchy for cats

Descent with modification explains the natural clustering of species into nested groups.

Pillar of Evidence 6: Molecular Similarities among Organisms

Modern molecular data provide an entirely new line of evidence in support of evolution. During the past 40 years, scientists have invented ways of measuring the similarity of molecules in different species. They use molecular and computer-based technologies to make the measurements. These measurements support, in an independent way, inferences Darwin made about descent with modification using other types of evidence. Whenever independent lines of evidence support the same conclusion, they strengthen it.

Descent from common ancestors explains the similarities in the DNA and proteins among different species. The degree of similarity indicates how closely related species are. The more closely related two species are, the more recently they diverged from a common ancestor.

Similarities among Molecules Reveal Evolution

Hemoglobin is the molecule in the blood of animals that transports oxygen. The molecule is made up from two types of proteins (an alpha protein and a beta protein). Proteins are made up of amino acids. The alpha protein in hemoglobin contains 141 amino acids; the beta protein contains 146 amino acids.

By comparing the amino acid sequences of hemoglobin from different species, scientists can determine how closely related they are. Recall that in biology, "related" means connected by a common ancestor. The data table shows how similar human hemoglobin is to hemoglobin from several other species.

Species Comparison	Percent Similar	
	Alpha Protein	Beta Protein
Human-Chimpanzee	100%	100%
Human-Rhesus Monkey	97%	95%
Human-Horse	87%	83%
Human-Frog	No data	54%
Human-Carp	50%	No data

Similarity of Human Hemoglobin to Hemoglobin in Other Species

The data in the following table show similar results for cytochrome c, an energy-producing protein found in the mitochondria of animals, plants, and fungi.

Species Comparison	Percent Similar
Human-Rhesus Monkey	99%
Human-Horse	88%
Human-Bullfrog	83%
Human-Fruit Fly	73%
Human-Wheat Plant	62%
Human-Neurospora Fungus	56%

Similarity of Human Cytochrome C to Cytochrome C in Other Species

Look at the next table. The data for DNA comparisons also show similarities.

Species Comparison	Percent Similar
Human-Chimpanzee	91%
Human-Rat	78%
Human-Horse	78%
Human-Frog	77%
Human-Fruit fly	74%
Human-Yeast	Not significant

Similarity of Human Mitochondrial DNA (mDNA) to mDNA in Other Species

The overall percentage of similarity between two species based on molecular evidence varies somewhat depending on which molecules are used for the test.

Descent with modification from common ancestors explains the striking molecular similarities among diverse species.

Finally, all life-forms have DNA and RNA as their genetic material. They share the same genetic code (with minor exceptions in mitochondria and some microorganisms) and certain identical biochemical pathways. They inherited these molecular traits from the most ancient common ancestor of living things. This ancestor was a bacterium that lived about 3.5 billion years ago.

Pillar of Evidence 7: Direct Observation of Ongoing Evolution

Although Darwin did not directly observe a natural population evolve, modern scientists have observed evolutionary change occurring in a wide variety of species that have short generation times, including bacteria, fruit flies, birds, and fish. Change has occurred in the physical, molecular, behavioral, and genetic makeup of populations living in the laboratory and in the wild in as a short a time as a year or less. Widespread medical use of antibiotics is encouraging the evolution of dangerous disease pathogens. You will learn more about this evidence of evolution in the next three chapters.

The Weight of Evidence

During his five-year voyage on the *Beagle*, young Charles Darwin made many observations that challenged his ideas about the living world. Within two years after his return, he worked out his ideas about biological evolution. Central to his thinking was the idea that species arise by descent with modification from common ancestors.

Darwin's new idea was logical and it accounted for life on Earth using only natural processes (two of the criteria of scientific explanations). But Darwin knew that a scientific explanation also must be supported by evidence and it must make verifiable predictions. He spent the next 20 years collecting further evidence and found that this evidence also supported his ideas.

Finally, Darwin assembled the many lines of evidence that supported his idea and published them in his book *On the Origin of Species*. The book presents evidence from the first five pillars you studied in this chapter. As you discovered, his simple, powerful idea—descent with modification—explains many otherwise puzzling observations about life: the fossil record, the structural similarities among organisms, the geographic distribution of organisms, the embryological similarities among organisms, and the natural

Scientists have observed evolution in Darwin's finches on the Galápagos Islands.

pattern of organism groupings. Observations in each of these areas independently support the theory of evolution.

Since Darwin's time, scientists have discovered additional evidence within each of the first five pillars. In addition, two new pillars provide additional support—evidence from molecular similarities among organisms and direct observations of evolutionary change within species. The theory of evolution is an extraordinarily well-supported explanation for the origin of diversity, unity, and adaptations that we observe among Earth's millions of species.

The evidence that supports the theory of evolution has led scientists to conclude that (**1**) species evolve across time; (**2**) the great diversity of organisms is the result of more than 3.5 billion years of evolution; (**3**) the millions of different plants, animals, fungi, and microorganisms that live on Earth are related by descent from common ancestors; (**4**) organisms are classified into a hierarchy of groups and subgroups based on similarities that reflect their evolutionary relationships; and (**5**) descent from common ancestors explains the fossil record and the similarities (unity) among Earth's diverse species. ●

"The basic theory of evolution has been confirmed so completely that modern biologists consider evolution simply a fact."

Ernst Mayr, biologist,
Harvard University

The Genetic Basis
of Evolution

hen Charles Darwin published *On the Origin of Species* in 1859, he presented evidence that the physical characteristics of species change across time, that is, evolve. Chance variations provided raw material for evolution, but he did not know the mechanism by which variation arose. About 50 years after Darwin's death, scientists rediscovered the earlier and obscure work of geneticist Gregor Mendel.

In the 1930s and 1940s, scientists combined Darwin's ideas about evolution with Gregor Mendel's ideas about genetics and created the modern theory of evolution. It explains how the characteristics of populations change across time, including their genetic characteristics. In fact, scientists now know that genetic changes are the basis for changes in observable characteristics. To understand how this happens, you need to understand something about population genetics.

Before you learn about population genetics, stop and look at the picture on this page. What big idea about the modern theory of evolution does this picture communicate to you? Be ready to discuss your interpretation. You'll get another chance to interpret this picture at the end of the chapter.

"Darwin and his contemporaries worked without any real knowledge of genetics. Then Mendel's basic laws were rediscovered about the turn of the 20th century. Combined with identification of chromosomal structure and function and, finally, the elegant statistical formulations of population genetics, the modern synthetic theory of evolution was established."

David Barash,
biologist

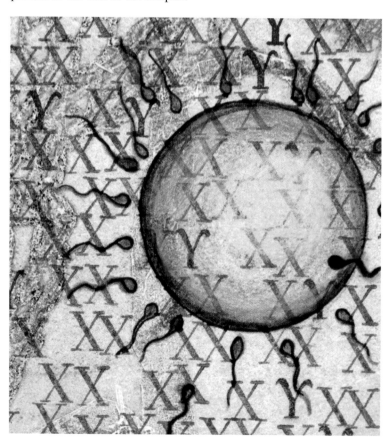

Introduction to Population Genetics

You are already familiar with the genetics of individuals. Individual animals, plants, fungi, and single-celled eukaryotes (such as *Paramecium*) have two sets of matching chromosomes inside the nuclei of their cells. Each set came from one of the organism's parents. Each chromosome is made up of DNA (the genetic material). Sections of DNA, known as genes, contain the information that codes for an individual's unique, genetically based characteristics (traits). In humans, such traits include eye color, hair color, skin color, and height.

A population is a group of organisms of the same species that inhabit an area. They are members of the same species because they can mate with one another and produce healthy offspring. If you make a list of the genes for each individual in a population, then combine the lists, you will have what scientists call the population's *gene pool*. Let's look at the gene pool for a population of 100 imaginary annual plants. Annual plants live only one year and die after reproducing.

Imagine that each plant's DNA contains about 30,000 genes (for example, gene *A*, gene *B*, gene *C*, *D*, *E*, and so on, for all 30,000 genes). The diagram shows the genetic makeup (genotype) of the plants for one of these 30,000 genes—gene *A*. Gene A determines flower color. This gene exists in the population in two forms, or variants, *A* and *a*. Different forms of a gene are called *alleles*.

Assume that in this species, individuals with *AA* or *Aa* genotypes produce red flowers. Individuals with an *aa* genotype produce white flowers. So gene *A* produces two phenotypes (that is, two observable traits) in this species—red flowers and white flowers—depending on which alleles are present. If a plant has at least one copy of the *A* allele present, this allele directs the cells that form the petals of the flower to manufacture a red pigment. If no *A* allele is present, no pigment is produced.

You can now describe the genetic makeup of the population for this gene and determine whether the gene pool is changing from one generation to the next. This is important because scientists often define evolution as change in the genetic makeup of a population.

Assume that 49 plants in the 100-plant population have the genotype *AA*. This means that the genotype frequency of *AA* in the population is 49 percent *AA* (49 out of 100). Assume also that the frequencies of the other genotypes are 42 percent *Aa* (42 out of 100) and 9 percent *aa* (9 out of 100). The phenotype frequencies

White-flowered columbine (top) and red-flowered columbine (bottom)

are 91 percent red-flowered plants (49 + 42 out of 100) and 9 percent white-flowered plants (9 out of 100).

Plant Population (100 Plants)		Frequencies	Allele Frequencies
		Genotypes Phentotypes	
	49 AA plants (red)	AA = 49%	
			A = 70%
		91%	
	42 Aa plants (red)	red Aa = 42%	a = 30%
	9 aa plants (white)	Aa = 9% ......▶ 9% white	

The gene pool of this population of 100 individuals is composed of 200 alleles—140 *A* alleles and 60 *a* alleles. The frequencies of these alleles are 70 percent *A* (140 (200 = 0.70) and 30 percent *a* (60 (200 = 0.30). Make sure you understand how these frequencies were calculated. If you are not certain, count the number of *A* and *a* alleles for all individuals in the population.

Now that you have described the genetic makeup of the population, you can determine whether it is changing from generation to generation—that is, evolving. Scientists have discovered that the allele frequencies, the genotype frequencies, and the phenotype frequencies of a population will *stay the same* from one generation to the next unless one or more evolutionary forces cause them to change. What are these forces? The primary forces are (**1**) natural selection, (**2**) gene flow, (**3**) genetic drift, and (**4**) mutation. Let's look at how these forces can change the genetic makeup of a population.

Natural Selection as an Evolutionary Force

Imagine that a herd of deer wanders into an area where a population of 100 plants is living. If the deer are attracted to red flowers and eat 75 percent of the red-flowered plants and none of the white-flowered plants, the genetic makeup of the population changes. Now, only 12 *AA* plants and 11 *Aa* red-flowered plants are alive, but all 9 *aa* white-flowered plants are alive.

The total number of alleles in the surviving population of 32 plants is now 64. There are 35 *A* alleles (24 from *AA* individuals

+ 11 from *Aa* individuals) and 29 *a* alleles (18 from *aa* individuals + 11 from *Aa* individuals). The allele frequencies are 55 percent *A* (35 (64) and 45 percent *a* (29 (64).

The genetic makeup of the next generation will change too. If the 32 survivors mate randomly, produce 100 offspring, then die, the genotype frequencies of the next generation will be 30 percent *AA*, 50 percent *Aa*, and 20 percent *aa*. To learn how these new genotype frequencies are calculated, zoom in on the next generation.

How did the genotype and phenotype makeup of the population change? How might this population continue to evolve if the deer returned year after year to browse? Scientists can use mathematical formulas to predict the genetic makeup of populations from generation to generation.

In this example, deer were a selective force that caused the traits of the plant population to evolve. Many living and nonliving environmental factors, such as temperature, moisture, and various life-sustaining resources (such as food) also can act as selective forces. For example, individuals who have certain inherited traits that allow them to obtain food more efficiently are likely to produce more offspring over their lifetimes than individuals who lack these traits. Across time, the frequency of individuals with these traits in a population will increase. This is because natural selection is differential reproduction. Differential reproduction is the ability of individuals with certain advantageous traits to produce more offspring than other individuals under particular environmental conditions. Which trait was advantageous in our example? How did the frequency of that trait change?

Selection occurs because individuals vary in their traits, and some variations give individuals a reproductive advantage over others. Across time, these individuals contribute more offspring to the population. This causes the frequency of favorable traits in the population to increase and makes the population increasingly adapted to its environment.

You will see some real-life examples of natural selection in action in the next chapter. For now, the important point to remember is that natural selection is one force that causes populations to evolve. It's also an important force because it leads to adaptation.

Populations evolve through natural selection because better-adapted individuals are naturally selected by the environment. This means that, on average, they contribute more offspring to the next generation than individuals who are less well adapted

Zoom in on the offspring in the next generation.

TAKE CHARGE
OF YOUR LEARNING

Calculate the percent change in the genotype (*AA*, *Aa*, and *aa*), allele (*A* and *a*), and phenotype (red plants, white plants) frequencies between the generations. Record this information in your notebook.

Natural selection causes populations to evolve.

to the environment. Across time, natural selection alters the genetically influenced traits of a population. The population can be as small as a group of plants living in part of a forest or as big as an entire species.

Variation Is Necessary for Natural Selection to Occur

As you learned in Chapter 2, natural selection occurs because individuals vary in the degree to which they are adapted to their environment. Individuals whose traits make them better adapted to the environment tend to be naturally selected. That is, they tend to contribute more offspring to future generations than individuals who are less well adapted, and they pass these traits to their offspring through inheritance. Across time, this causes the traits of a population to change, with adaptive traits becoming more frequent.

Individual Variation

All individuals of sexually reproducing species vary in their physical, physiological, biochemical, and behavioral traits. For example, plants vary in flower color, petal shape and size, leaf size, and many other physical traits. Much of the variation in populations is *continuous*. This means that there are small differences among individuals.

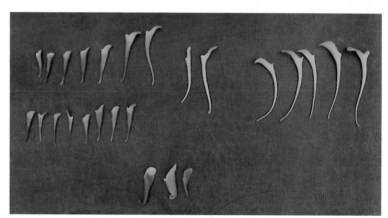

Variation in flower spur length within and among species of columbine. Each group of flower parts with the same color is from the same species.

So why do individuals have different traits? Why, for example, do humans have different skin and eye colors? Why does flower color vary within some plant species? Why do individuals of a species have slightly different physiologies and behavioral tendencies?

Activity:
Simulating Genetic Change through Natural Selection

All members of a species vary in their traits.

Zoom in on variation in animals.

The Cause of Variation

Most of the variation you see among individuals in a population is due partly to the influence of genes and partly to the influence of the environment. Only traits whose variability has a genetic component are important in evolution because the variation can be passed from parents to offspring.

Genetic recombination during meiosis is an important source of variation in populations of sexually reproducing species. This means that each individual's gametes (sex cells such as eggs or sperm) contain different combinations of their alleles.

When the gametes from different individuals combine, the offspring receives half of its alleles from each parent. This means that all of the offspring of two parents will be different from each other genetically (unless they are identical twins). To see why, consider the following 1-gene, 2-gene, 5-gene, and 50-gene examples.

If two individuals with Aa genotypes mate, they can produce 3 types of offspring (*AA*, *Aa*, and *aa*). If two individuals with *AaBb* genotypes mate, they can produce 9 types of offspring. If two individuals with *AaBbCcDdEe* genotypes mate, they can produce 243 types of offspring. If two individuals with 50-gene genotypes mate, they can produce 700,000,000,000,000,000,000,000 types of offspring. Now imagine how many types of offspring two individuals with 30,000 genes (such as humans) can produce. The number is astronomical! Even the simplest plants, animals, and fungi have thousands of genes.

Mutations and gene flow also produce variation, but variation from these sources is usually less important over short spans of time such as a generation.

The Connection between Genes and Traits

To see how genes produce observable variation, consider a plant in which seed production is genetically based. Assume for a moment that the imaginary plant we looked at earlier has a gene that controls seed production (gene *B*). If two individuals with the genotype *Bb* mate, they can produce three genotypes of offspring, each producing a different seed number phenotype. Some genotypes are more likely to occur than others. Study the following data table, then answer the questions that follow.

● **TAKE CHARGE**
OF YOUR LEARNING

Look closely at your classmates. Describe the variation you see for two traits.

Zoom in on how many types of offspring can be produced.

Genotype and Seed Production

Genotypes of Possible Offspring	Percent of Offspring with Genotype	Number of Seeds Genotype Produces
BB	25	4
Bb	50	2
bb	25	0

What is the relationship between genotype and seed production in this plant? Which allele controls seed production?

If you went out in nature and counted the seeds produced by 200 of these plants, you would likely collect the data shown in the following graph. How would you describe seed number variation in this population?

Seed Production (1 Gene)

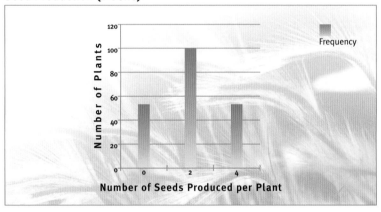

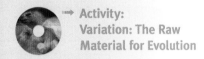

⟹ **Activity:**
Variation: The Raw
Material for Evolution

Now assume that two genes (*B* and *C*) control seed production. If two individuals with *BbCc* genotypes mate, they can produce

Seed Production (2 Genes)

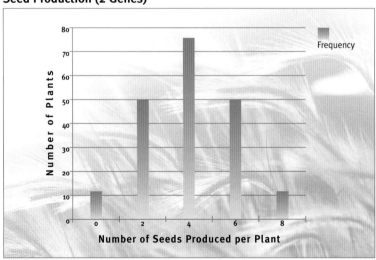

nine genotypes of offspring. If seed production is the same as in the previous example, the graph on page 70 shows the data you would likely collect from a population of 200 plants. When the two genes described are involved, the number of phenotypes (five) is less than the number of genotypes (nine).

How would you describe seed number variation in this population? How does it compare with the previous graph? What do you think the variation would look like if three genes controlled seed production?

Variation and Evolution

What does this all mean? It means that all individuals in real populations are genetically and phenotypically unique. Individuals will vary in their ability to contribute offspring to the next generation based partly on their genetic makeup. This variation is the raw material for natural selection. Natural selection favors the increase of alleles that promote reproductive success. Changes in the gene pool due to natural selection can cause changes in the observable characteristics of the population.

Variation is the raw material for evolution.

Gene Flow as an Evolutionary Force

Scientists have observed that nearly all water snakes (Nerodia sipedon) living along the shoreline of western Lake Erie have a dark-banded color pattern. Most of them living on islands within the lake are lighter colored and have reduced or no banding. Scientists asked the question, What is the explanation for this difference? One hypothesis is natural selection.

Field experiments show that unbanded snakes living on the light-colored rocks of island shorelines are better camouflaged against predators than banded snakes, and they have a higher survival rate. Banded snakes, on the other hand, are better camouflaged in the dense marshland vegetation that grows along the shoreline of the lake. Use your knowledge of evolution to figure out how the color pattern difference between the mainland and island snake populations could develop as the result of natural selection caused by predators.

Scientists then asked, If natural selection favors unbanded snakes on the islands, why aren't all snakes on these islands unbanded? The answer is gene flow. Genetic studies show that in every generation, several snakes migrate from the mainland to the islands and breed with the island snakes. Because most migrants are banded,

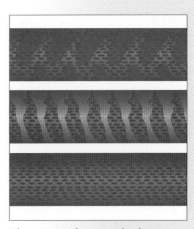

The patterns of water snakes living on the mainland and islands of western Lake Erie

Snails disperse shorter distances than fruit flies.

Dispersal of *Drosophila pseudoobscura* Fruit Flies Two Days after Release

Distance from Release Point (Meters)	Number of Flies
Near release point	123
80	116
160	67
240	67
320	45
400	35
480	11
560	2
640	3
720	6
800	2

they introduce their alleles for banded coloration into the island population's gene pool. These migrants make up about 1 percent of the island's snake population. These investigations show that variation in the color pattern of water snakes results from the combined effects of natural selection and gene flow.

The genetic makeup of a population changes if individuals move into or out of the population. Individuals moving into a population bring their alleles into the population's gene pool; individuals moving out remove their alleles from the gene pool. Besides the movement of individuals, gene flow takes place when pollen grains, spores, or gametes move between populations. The flow of alleles into or out of a population changes the population's gene pool. Gene flow takes place because entities that carry alleles, such as individuals, pollen, and spores, can move between populations.

Dispersal

To get a handle on potential gene flow, scientists have measured the dispersal distances of various species. Dispersal refers to the distance that organisms move from their point of origin or release. How would you collect data on the dispersal distances of animals such as fruit flies and snails?

Scientists have discovered that some species disperse longer distances than others. For example, the average *Drosophila pseudoobscura* fruit fly moves about 200 to 300 meters (650 to 1,000 feet) per generation; the lizard *Lacerta* moves 31 meters (100 feet); the snail *Cepaea* moves 8 meters (26 feet); and *Phlox* plant seeds move 1 meter (3 feet).

There is also a pattern to the dispersal tendencies of individuals of a species. When you study the dispersal data for fruit flies shown at right, how far did most of the flies move from the release point? What does the number of flies found at different distances tell you about the dispersal tendencies of this species? What do these data tell you about the potential for gene flow among fly populations?

Genetic Change Due to Gene Flow

Scientists use mathematics to measure the effect of gene flow. They have discovered that two factors determine how much the gene pool of a population will change due to gene flow. The two factors are (**1**) the number of individuals moving into and out of a population across time and (**2**) allele frequency differences between the migrants and the population. Scientists have also discovered that gene flow between populations tends to make them more similar.

Do you think gene flow is occurring among human populations? What's your evidence? How do you think gene flow among human populations has changed during the last few hundred years?

Gene flow causes populations to evolve.

Genetic Drift as an Evolutionary Force

Cypress trees in southern California grow in small, isolated groves. If you look closely at the groves, you will notice that the trees in each grove look similar to each other but quite different from trees in other groves. How would you explain these differences?

Scientists have discovered that small, isolated populations of cypress trees in California, land snails in Europe, fruit flies in laboratories, and even human populations around the world are different due to *genetic drift*. Genetic drift refers to random changes in allele frequencies due to chance. These random changes sometimes result in alleles disappearing from a population. The smaller the population, the more likely the gene pool will change due to genetic drift.

For example, if everyone in a group of people flips a coin 100 times, most people will get around 50 heads and 50 tails. The deviations from the expected 50:50 ratio are due to chance. With a large number of flips, most of the deviations from 50:50 will be small. But if everyone flips a coin only 10 times, there will be larger deviations from 50:50 due to chance. In fact, a few people might even get 10 heads and 0 tails, which is like losing their "tails" allele.

The same thing happens in populations. Scientists can estimate the percentage of offspring with particular genotypes that will be born to a set of parents. For example, the following diagram shows that 50 percent of the children born to *AA* and *Aa* parents will be *AA*, and 50 percent will be *Aa*. If these parents produce 100 children, the offspring genotypes (like the coins) will most likely

Genetic drift causes populations to evolve.

● TAKE CHARGE OF YOUR LEARNING

Flip a coin 10 times and record your results. Flip it 10 more times, then 10 times again. How much did your 10-flip trials vary from a 50:50 ratio? Add up the results of the 30 flips. Is your result closer to 50:50? Explain your results.

	Parent Aa	
	A	a
Parent AA	AA (50%)	Aa (50%)

be close to 50:50. If, however, they produce only 10 children, it is more likely that the offspring genotypes will deviate further from 50:50 due to chance combinations of different male and female gametes. They might even produce 10 *AA* children and 0 *aa* children.

Genetic Drift in the Laboratory

Scientists have observed drift occurring in the laboratory. For example, one team of scientists created 96 separate populations made up of eight fruit flies each (four males and four females) to study the effect of genetic drift on the frequencies of bristle alleles. Bristles are hairlike structures on a fruit fly's body.

At the beginning of the experiment, the frequency of the allele for straight bristles (*F*) in the gene pool was 50 percent. The fre-

Forked (left) and straight (right) bristles in fruit flies

quency of the forked bristle allele (*f*) was also 50 percent. After reproduction occurred, scientists randomly selected four males and four females to become the parents of the next generation. They continued this for 16 generations and discovered that one of the alleles (either F or *f*) had disappeared from the gene pool in 70 of the 96 populations. The alleles disappeared because, by chance, the parents chosen to create the next generation lacked one of the alleles and could not pass it on to the next generation.

Genetic Drift in the Wild

Genetic drift has been detected in many natural populations too. For example, there are two small populations of Torrey pine in southern California. One population is located near San Diego and

A Torrey pine

contains about 3,000 trees. The other is located 280 kilometers (174 miles) away on Santa Rosa Island and contains 2,000 trees.

The trees within each population are nearly identical, but look different from the trees in the other population. Biochemical evidence shows the same thing. All of the trees within each population are genetically identical for 59 enzyme genes, but differ from the trees in the other population for two of the enzyme genes.

The small genetic difference between these two tree populations is probably due to genetic drift rather than natural selection or gene flow. Genetic and biogeography evidence suggest that the island population formed from the dispersal of a small number of seeds produced by mainland trees. Because the founding population was small, its gene pool, by chance, did not have the same alleles present as the larger population. This founding population contained the parents of the trees found today.

Believe it or not, scientists have also discovered genetic drift in human populations. Throughout history, humans in many parts of the world have lived in small, somewhat isolated populations of 200 to 500 adults. The genetic makeup of such populations can change from generation to generation due to genetic drift.

For example, scientists once discovered a small group of about 270 Inuits living in a remote part of northern Greenland near

An Inuit

Blood-type Allele Frequencies in Greenland Eskimo Populations

Population	Allele Frequency (percent)		
	I^A	I^B	I^O
South of Nanortalik	35	5	60
Cape Farewell	33	3	64
Jakobshavn	29	5	66
Thule	9	3	84

Thule. Compare the blood type (A, B, and O) allele frequencies (I^A, I^B, and I^O) of the Inuit populations shown in the table. Natural selection does not seem to be acting on the blood type alleles in the Thule population. Why do you think scientists suspect that genetic drift occurred in the Thule population? How would the northern population's gene pool likely change if individuals from other populations migrated there?

Mutation as an Evolutionary Force

Did you know that you are a mutant? Don't be alarmed, everyone is. Everyone has cells whose DNA has a few mutations present.

Fortunately, most mutations are not lethal. In fact, some are beneficial. Mutations are one of the reasons why everyone is genetically unique. The occurrence of mutations causes the gene pool of a population to change across time.

What Is a Mutation?

A mutation is a spontaneous change in an organism's genetic material (DNA). Mutations are caused by DNA copying errors and by environmental factors such as radiation.

The most common mutation is called a *point* or *gene mutation*. Point mutations are molecular changes in the nucleotide base sequence of a gene. Such mutations often alter an organism's observable traits (its phenotype).

For example, a particular gene may have somewhere along its length a three-base sequence (cytosine-thymine-thymine [CTT]) that codes for the amino acid glutamic acid. Recall that genes code for proteins, and proteins are composed of amino acids. This sequence could mutate to guanine-thymine-thymine (GTT). Such a mutation would cause the cell to substitute the amino acid glutamine in the protein instead of glutamic acid. This change could affect the protein's functioning, which could change the organism's phenotype. Because of this change, scientists consider the gene a mutant allele. There are other types of mutations too.

Mutations can occur in the DNA of any cell of your body. Many of these mutational changes are not heritable, so they will not be passed to your offspring. However, if a mutation occurs in a cell that produces eggs or sperm, then you can pass this mutant allele to your offspring.

Mutations occur in all species, and any gene can mutate. Scientists have discovered mutations that affect a variety of traits. For example, scientists have discovered mutations in fruit flies that affect the wings, bristles, eyes, body color, and many other traits. The same is true for the traits of plants, such as leaf shape.

Some mutations have minor effects; some have major effects. In fruit flies, for instance, minor mutations change the number of bristles on the body. But there is also a major mutation that changes the number of wings from two to four. The important point to remember is that a mutation can change the type of protein an organism produces, which can change the phenotype.

Mutation Rates

The mutation rate for particular genes is low. For example, the mutation for albinism (the inability to produce pigmentation in the skin, hair, and eyes) in humans is found in 3 of every 100,000 gametes. In fruit flies, the mutation for yellow body color occurs in 12 of every 100,000 sex cells. One in every million gametes in corn has the mutation that produces shrunken seeds. One in every hundred million bacteria has a mutation that makes it resistant to the antibiotic streptomycin.

Although the mutation rate for particular genes is low, populations in nature can be large. Large populations produce large numbers of sex cells (gametes), so mutations are present in each generation of sperm and eggs. This is why mutation is a source of variation in populations.

An albino squirrel

The Effects of Mutations

Research on fruit flies has shown that about 90 percent of mutations have negative effects on individuals. This is because natural selection has been adapting species for millions of years (if not longer), so most random changes (particularly big ones) that occur in the DNA have negative effects. Fortunately, most harmful mutations have only slightly negative effects. Surprisingly, about 10 percent of the mutations in fruit flies have beneficial effects. Mutations can be neutral too.

Another thing to remember is that the adaptive value of a mutation depends on the organism's environment. For example, scientists once discovered that a particular mutation in fruit flies reduced survival at one temperature, but increased survival at a different temperature. Depending on the environment, mutation can be the starting point for evolutionary change. It is also important to remember that beneficial mutations occur by chance; they do not occur in response to the needs of the organism.

Mutations and Evolutionary Change

Both minor and major mutations play a role in evolution, although data indicate that minor mutations are more important. If a minor mutation has positive effects that give individuals greater reproductive success, natural selection will cause the frequency of the mutant allele to increase in the gene pool.

Keep in mind that when a mutant allele first appears in an individual, the odds are high that it will disappear in the population

Mutations cause populations to evolve.

by chance alone. Scientists estimate that the probability of a neutral mutant allele surviving one generation is about 63 percent. The probability of the allele surviving 127 generations is only 2 percent. Even if the allele gives the individual a 1 percent survival advantage over other individuals, the probability of the allele surviving 127 generations is low (only 3 percent).

All of this means that mutations are not usually a major evolutionary force for changing the genetic makeup of a population from one generation to the next. Mutation rates are low, so mutation alone does not bring about big changes in a population's gene pool. Furthermore, most mutations have negative effects, so they are likely to be eliminated from the population. However, mutation is important as the ultimate source of new variation in a population. Scientists call mutations the ultimate source of variation because mutations produce new alleles that recombine with other alleles during meiosis, which are then acted upon by natural selection.

The Genetic Basis of Evolution in a Nutshell

Scientists often define evolution as a change in the genetic makeup of a population. The genetic makeup of a population will stay the same from generation to generation unless one or more forces cause it to change. These forces are natural selection, gene flow, genetic drift, and mutation. When are these forces acting? Always!

Scientists do not know of any situation in nature or in the laboratory when one or more of these forces is not acting. This means that every population is constantly evolving because these forces are always at work changing the population's gene pool. This, in turn, can cause the population's observable traits to change. The most important evolutionary force is natural selection, but all evolutionary forces (gene flow, genetic drift, and mutations) cause populations to evolve. ●

All populations are constantly evolving.

Evolution in Action

Natural selection is the evolutionary mechanism that produces adaptive changes in populations across time.

How does evolution happen? How do populations and species change across time? You learned in Chapter 2 that Charles Darwin and Alfred Russel Wallace proposed that natural selection was the primary mechanism of evolution. Although natural selection is not the only way that evolution happens, most scientists today agree that natural selection is the most important mechanism for evolutionary change. This is because only natural selection changes populations in ways that better adapt them to their environment.

In *On the Origin of Species*, Darwin described evolution by *natural selection* as descent with modification. He could have said descent with *adaptive* modification. In this chapter, you will take a closer look at how natural selection works.

Discovering Natural Selection

Because natural selection is a process that changes populations gradually across many generations, it is not easy to observe. In fact, experimental evidence for it was not collected until the mid-1900s. Since then, many field and laboratory studies have demonstrated natural selection in action.

Darwin and Wallace independently uncovered the process of natural selection by observing and reasoning, rather than by direct experimentation. They observed that organisms were adapted to their surroundings and began looking for the cause of adaptation.

Each of these stick insects is adapted to its particular surroundings.

"Natural selection is at one and the same time a blind and a creative process . . . natural selection does not work according to a fore-ordained plan, and species are produced not because they are needed for some purpose but simply because there is an environmental opportunity and genetic wherewithal to make them possible."

Theodosius Dobzhansky, biologist

Darwin and Wallace collected some facts and then drew logical inferences, or conclusions, as to the likely cause of adaptive change within populations. Their answer was natural selection. Individuals who are better adapted to the environment tend to survive and reproduce more often than individuals who are less well adapted. This causes the characteristics of a population to change across time as the population becomes better adapted to its environment.

Across long periods of time, natural selection can change a population enough to create a new species.

Darwin's and Wallace's method of thinking is commonly used in the historical sciences. Historical sciences try to reconstruct past events. Darwin and Wallace reasoned backward from the effect (the adaptation of organisms) to a cause (natural selection). The biologist Thomas H. Huxley was so impressed by Darwin's reasoning that he wrote, "[Darwin] does not so much prove that natural selection does occur, as that it *must* occur." (italics added)

Scientists today can test the idea of natural selection by reasoning in the forward direction, *from* cause *to* effect. They then collect data to see whether their predictions are supported or refuted. For example, scientists studying medium ground finches on the Galápagos Islands might predict that average beak shape in the population will decrease from one generation to the next when small seeds are more abundant as food than large seeds are. They might predict this because finches with shallower beaks eat small seeds more efficiently and would likely survive and reproduce more often than finches with deeper beaks. Scientists could test this prediction by collecting data on beak size before and after weather conditions change the types of seeds available for the finches to eat.

What facts did Darwin and Wallace use to infer that natural selection occurred? They noticed that more individuals are born each generation than can survive and that each individual has unique heritable characteristics (or traits) that it can pass on to its offspring. Furthermore, some individuals have traits that make them better suited (adapted) to the environment than other individuals. Darwin and Wallace put these facts together and concluded that the result would be differential reproductive success among individuals—or natural selection.

Zoom in for a closer look at Darwin's thinking about natural selection.

➡ **Activity:**
Darwin's Solutions to the Puzzle of Evolution

Natural Selection: The Mechanism for Adaptive Evolutionary Change

Three conditions cause natural selection to occur. First, not all offspring born into a population survive and reproduce because limited resources (such as food and shelter), predators, disease, and environmental stresses cause many of these offspring to die. Second, individuals vary in their traits, and some of this variation is heritable. Third, some variations give individuals a survival and reproductive advantage.

Chapter 5

Because these conditions apply in nature at all times, the most likely outcome whenever organisms interact with each other and the physical environment is natural selection. Individuals with heritable advantages produce, on average, more offspring who inherit these advantages. Across time, the proportion of advantaged individuals in the population increases. This means that populations are almost always undergoing adaptive change to their environment.

Natural Selection Affects Only Heritable Traits

Only traits that can be passed from one generation to the next through inheritance can be selected. Therefore, any trait that is influenced by genes is fair game for selection. This applies to most physical traits such as facial features, physiological traits such as immune function, and behaviors.

For example, beak size in medium ground finches is a heritable trait because it is genetically influenced. Birds with different beak sizes have different alleles influencing beak growth and pass these alleles to their offspring. This means that natural selection can modify beak size. As you will discover, scientists have observed beak size in this species evolve across time under the influence of natural selection.

Recall that Lamarck believed that traits acquired during life could be passed on to offspring. Today, scientists know that traits acquired during an individual's lifetime that are not genetically based cannot be selected because they are not heritable. Muscles bulked up by weight lifting, tattoos applied to the skin, and mutations in nonreproductive cells such as blood cells, are examples of nonheritable acquired traits. Mutations that occur in egg or sperm cells, however, can be selected because they are passed on through inheritance.

You might be surprised to learn that behaviors can evolve too. Each species behaves in ways that are typical for that species. Birds, for example, communicate using species-specific songs, spiders spin species-specific webs, and salmon migrate back to their birth streams during mating season. Both genes and environmental factors (such as learning and experience) contribute to the development of behavior in all species, but the relative contribution of each varies among and within species. For example, the behaviors of insects

TAKE CHARGE
OF YOUR LEARNING

People in Africa spray their houses with the insecticide DDT to kill malaria-carrying mosquitoes. One reason this spraying is controversial is because the mosquitoes might evolve resistance to DDT, as has been observed in house-flies. Use your knowledge of natural selection to explain how DDT resistance might evolve in mosquitoes.

Scientists have observed beak shape evolve in medium ground finches (Geospiza fortis) on the Galápagos Islands.

How do you think Lamarck explained the origin of the long neck in giraffes? How do you think modern scientists explain the origin of the long neck in giraffes?

are under greater genetic control than the behaviors of apes and humans. But even some human behaviors are genetically specified. The blink reflex is an example.

Behaviors differ in complexity and the amount of learning that is required. Instincts, such as singing in white-crowned sparrows, develop without prior experience, but can be fine-tuned through learning. Other behaviors require more learning. Young chimpanzees learn, for example, how to use twigs to fish tasty ants out of ant nests by watching older chimps and by practicing.

The point is that behaviors can evolve if natural selection can modify the genetically influenced, heritable structure of the brain and nervous system that underlies the behavior. This is not surprising because behavioral differences can greatly affect reproductive success among individuals. Individuals that respond more appropriately to predators, food, or members of their own species are more likely to survive and reproduce.

Behaviors can evolve if natural selection modifies the brain and nervous system.

Think of a feeding or reproductive behavior that you have seen in a wild animal. How might differences in this behavior among animals affect their survival and reproductive success?

Individuals Are Selected, but Populations Evolve

To understand how evolution takes place, you need to think in terms of populations, not individuals. A population is a group of individuals of one species that lives and reproduces in a particular area. Wildebeests living in the savanna of Kenya are a population, as are medium ground finches living on the Galápagos island of Daphne Major. Human beings living in North America are also a population.

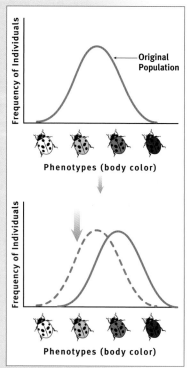

Frequency of Individuals

Original Population

Phenotypes (body color)

Frequency of Individuals

Phenotypes (body color)

The operation of natural selection is measured by change in the makeup of a population. The population changes gradually as individuals with favorable traits become more common across generations. How did the beetle body color in this population change from generation 1 (upper graph) to generation 2 (lower graph)?

TAKE CHARGE
OF YOUR LEARNING

Identify the three conditions that were present for natural selection to occur in the Galápagos finches. Then explain in your own words how shallower beaks evolved during wet years.

Individuals in a population live, reproduce, and die, but they do *not* evolve. Only populations evolve. The traits of a population change from generation to generation under natural selection because some individuals survive and reproduce more often than other individuals. Scientists track evolutionary changes in a population by measuring its traits across time. They commonly measure changes in the proportion of particular physical, biochemical, physiological, behavioral, or genetic traits.

Evolutionary change due to natural selection can occur slowly or quickly. For example, researchers studying medium ground finches on the Galápagos island of Daphne Major observed changes in beak shape in just 18 months. A drought in 1976–1977 shifted the finches' food supply toward large, tough seeds. Birds with deeper beaks open these seeds more easily than birds with shallow beaks. The shift in the food supply favored individuals in the populations that had deep beaks. This feeding advantage gave the deeper-beaked birds a survival and reproductive advantage over individuals with more shallow beaks. After just one generation, the finch population contained relatively more deep-beaked adult birds plus their deep-beaked offspring. This caused average beak depth to increase.

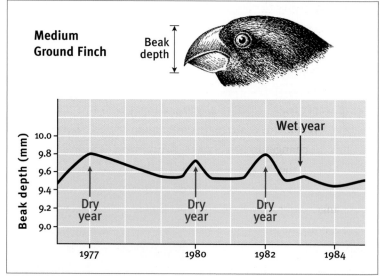

The graph shows evolutionary changes in beak depth in medium ground finches on the Galápagos island of Daphne Major under different environmental conditions. How much did average beak depth change between dry years and wet years in the 1980s and 1990s?

Scientists observed small evolutionary changes in beak depth in Galápagos finches in less than two years. More extensive evolutionary changes, like those that transformed some land mammals into whales, take millions of years.

Natural Selection Adapts Populations to the Environment

Natural selection is a process that adjusts populations to changing environmental conditions. Because the changes caused by natural selection depend upon environmental conditions, a trait that is advantageous in one environment might be disadvantageous in another. This means that the way any population adapts is not predetermined but depends on local conditions. For example, wet conditions on Daphne Major in 1993 resulted in more small seeds being produced. Now, shallower beaks were advantageous. How did beak depth change during the wet year?

Patterns of Natural Selection and Adaptive Change

Natural selection can produce three patterns of adaptive change in a population. These patterns are *directional selection*, *diversifying selection*, and *stabilizing selection*. In each case, selection changes the distribution of heritable variations in a population.

Directional Selection

When environmental conditions favor individuals having variations closer to one end of a variation spectrum, directional selection occurs. Directional selection shifts the distribution of the variations toward the favored direction. For example, it caused the shift toward deeper beaks in medium ground finches on Daphne Major during dry years. Directional selection commonly occurs when the environment changes in a consistent direction for a period of time.

Fossils from the ice age show that there was directional selection for larger body size in European bears during cold, glacial periods. This change might have been adaptive because larger mammals have less body surface area relative to their volume than smaller mammals. This means they lose body heat more slowly than smaller mammals. Larger bears therefore probably had a survival advantage during glacial periods because they conserved body heat better than smaller bears.

Environments are changeable, however, and sometimes shift back in the opposite direction. If this happens, individuals at the other end of a variation spectrum will be favored. Directional selection will reverse course and move a population's traits back

Evolution refers to change in the characteristics of a population across generations. Individual organisms do not evolve.

"It may be said that natural selection is daily and hourly scrutinizing, throughout the world, every variation, even the slightest; rejecting that which is bad; preserving and adding up all that is good; silently and insensibly working, whenever and wherever opportunity offers, at the improvement of each organic being in relation to its organic and inorganic conditions of life."

Charles Darwin, naturalist

Natural selection results in three patterns of adaptive change in populations: directional selection, diversifying selection, and stabilizing selection.

in the opposite direction. The bear fossil record shows a reversal in body size back to smaller bears during warm periods between glaciers. The shift back to shallower beaks in medium ground finches during wet years is another example of a reversal.

Diversifying Selection

When environmental conditions favor individuals at both ends of a variation spectrum over intermediate individuals, diversifying selection occurs. Diversifying selection tends to break a continuous distribution into two or more groups. Across time, diversifying selection can separate the groups until they become different species.

For example, stickleback fish found in certain lakes in the Canadian Rocky Mountains come in two forms. Each is at the far end of the distribution for body shape. One form has a stocky body with a large mouth that is suited for eating larger organisms that live in the sediment, such as worms. The other has a slender body with a small mouth that is suited for eating small prey swimming in the water. How do you think diversifying selection gave rise to these two forms of sticklebacks from an original population that also included intermediate forms?

Stabilizing Selection

When conditions favor individuals in the middle of a variation spectrum, stabilizing selection results. Stabilizing selection tends to keep the distribution of traits in a population constant and reduces the range of variation.

Mortality vs. Birth Weight

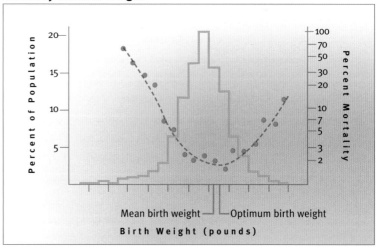

Stabilizing selection for birth weight in humans

Among human babies, for example, those weighing less than 2.7 kilograms (six pounds) or more than 3.6 kilograms (eight pounds) at birth have higher mortality than those weighing between 2.7 and 3.6 kilograms. Small babies are sometimes too underdeveloped to survive, whereas large babies sometimes suffer physical trauma during birth and have other medical problems. Stabilizing selection tends to keep the birth weight of human babies within this narrow range. Modern medicine has to some extent countered this example of stabilizing selection in humans. Many premature babies now survive with the help of technology, and Caesarean births reduce mortality among larger babies.

These three patterns of adaptive change demonstrate that natural selection is a dynamic process that responds to changing conditions. Yet in each case, selection operates the same way. Individuals with adaptive heritable variations have a reproductive advantage, so their descendants increase in frequency in the population.

Sexual Selection

Have you ever noticed that females and males of some sexually reproducing species look different? For example, male peacocks have brightly colored feathers, while the females are more drably colored. Male elk have antlers that females lack. Can you think of other species in which males look different from females?

Male-female differences in appearance and behavior are called sexual dimorphisms. They result from *sexual selection*. Sexual selection is a form of natural selection for traits that increase an individual's ability to obtain mates or the ability to choose well among potential mates. Sexual selection takes place whenever the individuals of one sex (usually males) compete among themselves for mating opportunities or when the individuals of one sex (usually females) choose among potential mates.

Male-male competition is a type of sexual selection. Here, males increase their reproductive success by competing with each other for territory and the opportunity to mate. During the mating season, for example, male elk joust with their antlers for the right to assemble a harem of females. Male giraffes fight each other with their necks for opportunities to mate. While Lamarck thought that giraffes acquired their long necks by stretching them to eat leaves high up in trees and then passing this acquired trait to their offspring, modern research suggests that long necks in giraffes evolved through sexual selection.

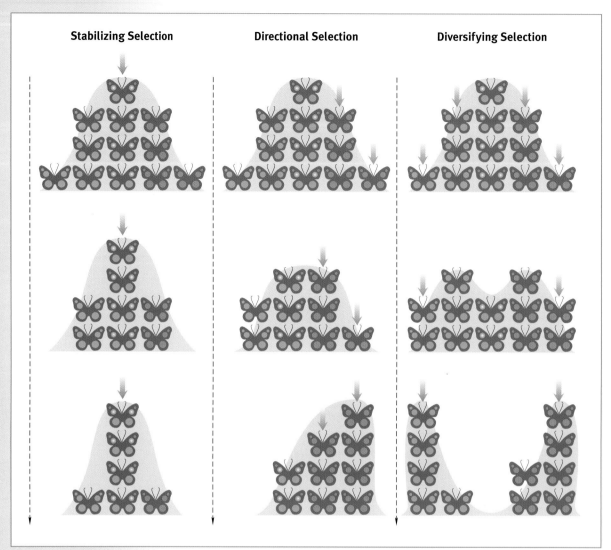

| Stabilizing Selection | Directional Selection | Diversifying Selection |

Butterflies vary in body color. The curves show how stabilizing (left), directional (center), and diversifying (right) selection can change the frequencies (percentages) of individuals of varying color in a population across time. The arrows point to body colors that are being selected for.

Giraffes with longer necks are more successful in fights and get greater access to females.

Female choice is another type of sexual selection in which females choose among "show-off" males. Males with certain attractive traits are more likely to be chosen by females as mates. For example, females are somewhat more likely to select male peacocks with longer feathers than males with shorter feathers. Scientists think that outlandish male adornments provide visual information about the male's "quality." Because females choose mates on the basis of certain traits, such as larger, more colorful feathers, these traits become more common among males in future generations.

Sexual selection explains how dimorphism between the sexes arises. It favors males who have traits that enhance their ability to attract or mate with many females. It favors females who are sexually discriminating and choose high-quality males. Across time, sexual selection results in males and females looking more and more different.

What Is a Species?

In his 1859 masterwork *On the Origin of Species by Means of Natural Selection*, Charles Darwin described how natural selection accounts for changes within populations and existing species. But as the book's title implies, he also said that natural selection explained the origin of *new* species. His phrase "descent with modification" summarized his conclusion that all new species arise from existing species and are modified in the process, primarily by natural selection. Unfortunately, Darwin had no detailed knowledge about how species form. Scientists today know a lot about the process called speciation.

Before we consider speciation, let's consider what a species is. Most people have a general understanding of what species are. They know, for example, that a mushroom and an oak tree are two different types of organisms (two species). But if we are to make meaningful comparisons among species, we need a more precise definition. Surprisingly, scientists have found it difficult to develop a single definition that can be used in all cases. Even Darwin's definition of a species was itself rather imprecise: "I look at the term species, as one arbitrarily given for the sake of convenience to a set of individuals closely resembling each other."

Darwin was nevertheless aware of a key characteristic of a species—members of the same species can interbreed in nature and produce fertile offspring. In the 20th century, biologist Ernst Mayr used interbreeding in a formal definition called the *biological species concept*. It defines a species as any population or group of populations whose members have the potential to interbreed with one another in nature to produce viable, fertile offspring. Organisms that cannot interbreed in nature to produce such offspring are said to be *reproductively isolated* and belong to different species.

This definition focuses on interbreeding rather than the extent to which organisms resemble one another. It is a useful concept because some organisms look alike but never interbreed in nature. They therefore belong to different species. For example, some fruit flies look nearly identical but never interbreed. On the other hand, some organisms look different but do interbreed. For instance,

Zoom in for a closer look at sexual selection in barn swallows.

The biological species concept is based on the ability of individuals to mate and produce fertile offspring rather than on physical similarity.

a

b

c

(a) Despite the great variation in their physical appearance, all dogs belong to the same species–Canis familiaris. (b) The Harris' antelope squirrel, Ammospermophilus harrisii, *and the white-tailed antelope squirrel,* Ammospermophilus leucurus *(insert), look similar in appearance but represent different species. They live on opposite sides of the Grand Canyon. (c) All humans belong to the same species* Homo sapiens.

various dog breeds look different but they interbreed, so they are members of the same species, *Canis familiaris.* Likewise, all humans can mate and produce fertile offspring. This means that all humans are members of the same species, *Homo sapiens.*

Since members of different species do not interbreed, the genetic makeup (or gene pool) of each species remains separate from other species. In genetic terms, there is no gene flow, or exchange of genes, between species. Because species are reproductively isolated in this way, each evolves without genetic input from other species. For example, humans and chimps do not produce viable offspring together so their gene pools remain separate. The horse and donkey also are reproductively isolated, but here there is an interesting twist. Horses and donkeys can produce viable offspring called mules, but mules are sterile. Mules cannot produce offspring of their own or with either parent. Because mules are a reproductive dead end, the gene pools of horses and donkeys remain reproductively isolated.

As useful as the biological species concept is, it has limitations. For example, scientists cannot apply it to fossil organisms or those that reproduce asexually, such as bacteria. In these cases, they must rely on appearance. There also are situations where scientists do not know whether particular organisms ever interbreed in nature because they live in different habitats and do not come into contact. Consider lions, which live in open grasslands, and tigers, which live in forests. They live apart and do not interbreed in the wild. However, lions and tigers will mate and produce fertile offspring when brought together in a zoo. Since lions and tigers have at least the potential to breed in the wild, the biological species concept does not apply very well to them.

To solve such problems, scientists have proposed another definition of species—the *ecological species concept*. It defines a species in terms of its ecological niche, that is, its habitat, the environmental resources it uses, and its behaviors. Under this definition, lions and tigers are considered separate species because their habitats and behaviors, not reproductive incompatibility, keep them from interbreeding. The important point is that the basic evolutionary relatedness of all life means that every definition of species is bound to fail in at least some cases.

How Species Form

Scientists think that most speciation involves the temporary isolation of a population from its parental population. During this period of isolation, the genetic makeup of the two populations changes independently of each other due to mutation, genetic drift, and most importantly, natural selection. Eventually, the two populations may become so different that they cannot successfully interbreed, even if they have the chance.

How does reproductive isolation between populations develop? It develops when two or more populations of a single species become geographically separated from one another and begin to change. This process is called *geographic speciation*. Speciation is sometimes called splitting, branching, or diverging.

During geographic speciation, a population of one species becomes subdivided into two or more groups by some type of geographic barrier such as a river, a canyon, or an expanse of ocean. The barrier prevents individuals in one group from interbreeding with those of the other. This isolation prevents the groups from mixing genes. Across time, natural selection might adapt each group to its environment differently.

Horse

Mule

Donkey

Horses (Equus caballus) *and donkeys* (Equus asinus) *are separate species even though they can produce viable offspring—mules. Mules are sterile, however, so they are reproductive and evolutionary dead ends and do not fit the definition of a biological species.*

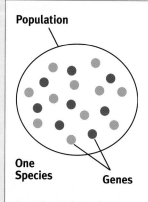
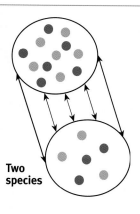
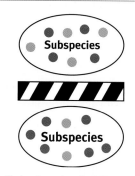
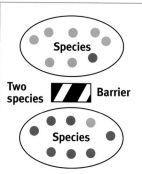

Population

One Species

Genes

A species made up of one interbreeding population consisting of individuals that show variation in their characteristics...

Two species

may in time expand its range and divide into two or more populations that have little gene exchange.

Subspecies

Subspecies

If a barrier to interbreeding arises, the gene pools are isolated. Through a very long period of time, mutation and selection make the different populations genetically distinct subspecies.

Species

Two species **Barrier**

Species

They may be considered separate species when they become so different that they can no longer interbreed even though little or no physical barrier remains.

Geographic isolation sometimes leads to reproductive isolation. Follow the sequence to see how this occurs. When the two populations become reproductively isolated, what has occurred?

For instance, directional selection might modify one group in one direction and another group in another direction. The groups may eventually come to differ so much physically or behaviorally that they do not interbreed even if the barrier is removed and the now-modified groups have contact with each other. If this happens, scientists call each group a different species because they are reproductively isolated from each other.

Evolutionary divergence between populations goes through a series of stages with time. For example, if an ancestral population splits into two isolated local populations, these populations may diverge genetically, physically, and behaviorally across time and become two subspecies, then two species, then perhaps even two genera. Genetic data supports this pattern of evolutionary change. One study of enzyme genes in fruit flies, for instance, showed that local populations were 97 percent similar, subspecies were 79 percent similar, sibling species (species that look nearly identical but do not interbreed) were 56 percent similar, and nonsibling species were only 35 percent similar.

Geographic speciation has been demonstrated in snapping shrimp (genus Altheus) living on the Atlantic and Pacific sides of the Isthmus of Panama. This isthmus is a narrow strip of land that connects North America to South America. Geological evidence indicates that North America and South America were once separated by ocean. Living in the ocean was a species of snapping shrimp. Following the emergence of the isthmus about 3 million years ago, the populations of snapping shrimp on the different sides of the isthmus began to evolve independently of each other.

DNA analysis shows that the snapping shrimp can be grouped into seven pairs of species, with one species of each pair found on each side of the isthmus. The DNA differences between the pairs range from 19 to 6.5 percent. The longer two populations have been separated, the more different they are genetically. Do the DNA data support the hypothesis that the isthmus formed all at once between North and South America or the hypothesis that it formed gradually? What is your reasoning?

Behavioral studies show that when males and females from different sides of the isthmus are placed together in aquariums, they do not produce fertile offspring. Do these data suggest that the snapping shrimp on different sides of the isthmus are the same or different species? What is your reasoning?

Speciation takes place in other ways too. It sometimes occurs when no geographic barriers separate populations, such as when ecological conditions favor individuals at the extreme ends of a variation spectrum. When this happens, diversifying selection can split a species into distinct groups with different physical characteristics. Across time, these groups may become separate species.

Recall the earlier example of the stickleback fish. The environmental conditions in the lake favored the evolution of big-mouthed fish and small-mouthed fish. In time, these fish might become separate species because they live in different habitats within the lake and seldom interbreed. Keep in mind that there is no geographic barrier between the populations. Instead, ecological or behavioral differences keep the two forms of fish apart. Each ended up specializing on particular foods for which it happened to be adapted. These differences translate into reproductive isolation between the groups. Since individuals tend to "hang out" and mate with members of their own group, the groups likely will become increasingly different across time and may become separate species.

Cichlid fishes in Lake Victoria in East Africa are another example of this type of speciation. Lake Victoria is a large lake that is less than a million years old. In this time, nearly 200 cichlid species have evolved in this single body of water. Since all of these fishes are closely related genetically, it is likely that they all evolved from one or a few ancestor species that first entered the lake during or shortly after it formed.

Across time, natural selection repeatedly subdivided the cichlid population into different groups that eventually became different species. Each species became specialized for exploiting different

TAKE CHARGE OF YOUR LEARNING

Recall that the white-tailed antelope squirrel and Harris' antelope squirrel look similar but represent different species living on opposite sides of the Grand Canyon. Explain how these two species likely evolved from the same ancestral species through the process of geographic speciation.

food and other resources in the lake. Some specialized on small fishes, others on free-floating microscopic plants and animals, others on organisms living in the pebbles at the bottom of the lake, and still others eating the scales off other fish.

The evolution of many diversely adapted species from a common ancestor species is called adaptive radiation. Other radiations include the evolution of 13 species of finches on the Galápagos Islands and more than 500 species of drosophilid flies (relatives of the fruit fly Drosophila) on the mountainsides of Hawaii. In both cases, geographic separation (different species found on different islands) and ecological specialization (different species found at different elevations on the same mountainside) played a role in speciation. These examples show that speciation is a process of repeated branching and diversification of new species from ancestral species. This process explains how species have multiplied to such a large number across time.

New species arise from existing species through the process of speciation. Speciation often, but not always, involves populations becoming geographically isolated from other populations and evolving independently of each other under the influence of natural selection and other evolutionary forces.

All 13 Galápagos finches (11 of which are pictured above) evolved from the same ancestral species through the process of adaptive radiation.

From Microevolution to Macroevolution

Evolutionary change takes place on several levels. These levels range from small changes in a population's genetic makeup to large changes in genetic makeup, appearance, and behavior. The term *microevolution* refers to small changes in the genetic makeup of a population that may or may not result in obvious changes in appearance and behavior. Such changes are sometimes detectable in as short a time as a few generations.

Macroevolution, on the other hand, refers to larger changes in genetic makeup, appearance, or behavior. Macroevolutionary changes are more complex and take millions of generations to accomplish. Such changes include the origin of the eukaryotic cell, multicellular organisms, limbs, and feathers. Scientists use novel features such as these to define taxonomic groups above the species level, such as particular orders, classes, and phyla.

Both microevolution and macroevolution rely on the same processes of evolutionary change—natural selection, mutation, genetic drift (random changes in gene frequencies due to chance), and migration. The difference between the two is that of degree. Many small changes can accumulate across large expanses of time to produce large, complex changes.

Think of species formation as being at the boundary between microevolution and macroevolution. For example, two species that recently diverged from their common ancestor are closely related and have only subtle differences between them. Such small differences may be the result of a few microevolutionary changes driven by natural selection and mutation. Species that diverged long ago, such as reptiles and mammals, are more distantly related and have had a much longer time period during which to accumulate additional changes. The cumulative modification of different groups across time adds up to macroevolutionary change.

Think back to the changes in beak shape that occurred in the medium ground finch on the Galápagos Islands. Was this an example of microevolutionary change or macroevolutionary change? What about the evolution of the two forms of stickleback in the lake in Canada?

Surprisingly, small changes at the genetic level can sometimes produce the large morphological changes seen in macroevolution. Such genetic changes typically occur in a relatively small number of regulatory genes that control embryological development. Many of these genes control either the timing of developmental events or the location where these events occur.

Changes in the timing of developmental events can cause large differences in the final form of an organism. For example, the faces of humans and chimps have a similar profile during the early fetal stage of development. As adults, however, their profiles are very different. How do they become different? The chimp's jaw grows faster during fetal development and after birth than the human jaw. As a result, the jaw in adult chimps ends up being much longer than in adult humans.

> Both microevolution and macroevolution rely on the same processes of evolutionary change. The difference between the two is a matter of degree. Many small changes can accumulate across time to produce large, complex changes.

⟹ Activity:
EvoDots: Modeling the Process of Evolutionary Change

The process that causes physical differences to arise between species due to differences in rates of development is called hete- rochrony. A relatively small number of genes, which are subject to natural selection and mutation, appear to control the timing of developmental events.

Large differences in body structure also can arise from mutation in genes that control where particular body parts form. So-called homeotic genes determine where body structures such as the head, limbs, wings, antennae, and backbones form. For example, certain *Hox* homeotic genes specify where legs develop in fruit flies. Mutations that cause these genes to be expressed in inappropriate locations, such as the head, result in flies growing legs on their head. If a different *Hox* gene is expressed in the wrong location, flies can develop a second pair of wings. Perhaps the most bizarre of all is when an eye-specifying homeotic gene called Pax 6 is activated inappropriately in the antenna-forming region of the head. This results in perfectly formed eyes developing on the surface of the antennae!

The particular homeotic mutations described above are not adaptive. In fact, they actually decrease reproductive success. The important point, however, is that large macroevolutionary changes in body organization can result from small changes in a few key regulatory genes that control embryological development. It is likely that during the evolutionary history of life, some homeotic changes of this kind were in fact advantageous and retained through natural selection.

As you read in Chapter 3, many important regulatory genes, including homeotic genes, are homologous across species. This means that genes with similar DNA sequences and functions are present in all multicellular organisms. For example, the same *Hox* genes that control the number and location of body segments in insects and worms also control the number and location of spinal column bones in humans. The earliest vertebrates (animals with backbones) inherited these regulatory genes from their invertebrate ancestors. Extra copies of these regulatory genes developed during DNA duplication, and natural selection then modified them. This allowed for more complex bodies to evolve.

These shared regulatory genes provide a mechanism for the evolution of more complex bodies during the history of life. Such homologies among regulatory genes are evidence of evolutionary relatedness among species and of descent with modification.

Mutations in a small number of regulatory genes affecting development can result in large changes in body organization.

Darwin's View of Evolution in Action

The following excerpt from Darwin's book *On the Origin of Species* summarizes his view of evolution. We added the bracketed words to make his writing easier to understand. What laws does he identify as leading to natural selection and adaptation? Why do you think he believes there is a splendor to this view of life?

It is interesting to contemplate a tangled bank, clothed with plants of many kinds, with birds singing on the bushes, with various insects flitting about, with worms crawling through the damp earth; and to reflect that these elaborately constructed forms, so different from each other, and dependent on each other in so complex a manner, have all been produced by laws [verifiable natural process] acting around us. These laws . . . being Growth [in population size, due to] Reproduction; Inheritance . . .; Variability [among individuals]; a ratio of [reproductive] increase so high as to lead to a Struggle for Life, and as a consequence to Natural Selection, [producing] Divergence of Character [descent with adaptive modification] and the extinction of [less-well-adapted] forms. Thus from the war of nature, from famine and death, the most exalted object which we are capable of conceiving, namely, the production of the higher animals, directly follows. There is a grandeur [splendor] in this view of life, with its several powers, having been originally breathed into a few forms or into one; and that, whilst this planet has gone cycling on according to the fixed law of gravity from so simple a beginning, endless forms most beautiful and most wonderful have been, and are being, evolved. ●

Zoom in on a detailed description of natural selection.

In the Light of Evolution

Chapter 6

The world-renowned biologist Theodosius Dobzhansky once said, "Nothing in biology makes sense except in the light of evolution." To understand what he means, consider the following observations about the living world:

- The same pattern of bones is found in the forelimbs of whales, horses, birds, and humans.

- The embryos of snakes, chickens, cats, and humans look similar during early stages of development.

- A 3.2-million-year-old fossil skeleton has an apelike head but a humanlike body.

- Human DNA is more similar to ape DNA than to fungus DNA.

How did scientists make these observations? How does your knowledge of evolution help you explain them? How might your knowledge of evolution help you understand the origin of humans?

In this chapter, we focus on human beings. We begin by looking at humans and their activities from an evolutionary perspective. We then examine some misunderstandings people have about evolution. Finally, we talk about people's growing understanding of the living world in the light of evolution.

Since this chapter focuses on humans, let's start at the beginning. How does science explain the origin of humans?

The Origin of Humans

How does the theory of evolution apply to our own species, *Homo sapiens*? If new species arise from other species, what species preceded us? Are they alive or extinct? Where did humans originate?

In his book *On the Origin of Species*, Charles Darwin said that "light will be thrown on the origin of man and his history" by his theory. In the mid-1800s, however, almost nothing scientific was known about human origins. Since then, scientists have added many lines of evidence—including fossils, body structure, biochemistry, DNA, and behavior—to a constantly growing body of knowledge about our origins. The power of this evidence has turned Darwin's "light" into a spotlight that illuminates the story of human evolution.

The theory of evolution helps us explain our observations about the living world.

"No biologist has been responsible for more—and for more drastic—modifications of the average person's worldview than Charles Darwin."

Ernst Mayr,
Harvard University biologist

Humanity's Place among the Animals

In Chapter 3, you saw how certain traits that humans share with certain other animals (for example, a backbone and mammary glands) identify us as vertebrates (subphylum Vertebrata) and as mammals (class Mammalia). Within the mammals, we humans and our close relatives are classified in the order Primates.

Examine the pictures of these primates. What observable traits do they have in common?

Humans and Apes

Scientists use fossil data, molecular comparisons, and body structures to construct evolutionary trees. Evolutionary trees show when different lines of descent (different lineages) formed. They also show how long each species has been changing in genetic isolation from other species. For example, scientists use the fact that a given gene's DNA mutates at a fairly constant rate to calculate a molecular clock of evolution. To understand what this means, zoom in on the molecular clock.

Zoom in on the molecular clock.

Scientists have concluded that the common ancestor of all primates was a mouselike animal that lived about 60 million years ago (MYA). Nearly 50 MYA, the primates split into three major lineages. Look at the following evolutionary tree and identify these lineages. Which lineage produced a group called the hominoids? The *hominoids* include apes (gibbons, orangutans, gorillas, and chimpanzees) and humans.

Recall that the more similar the DNA is between two species, the more closely related they are. Study the DNA data on p. 102. Which ape is most similar to humans? What can you conclude from these data? How does Darwin's idea of descent with modification from common ancestors explain these data?

Scientists use fossil data, molecular comparisons, and body structure comparisons to reconstruct evolutionary history.

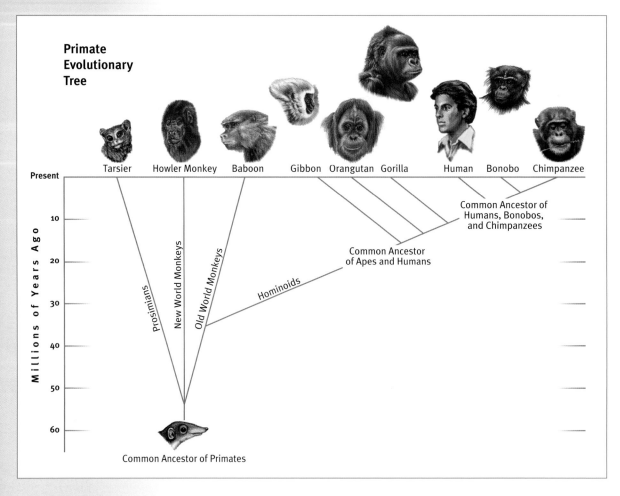

Primate Evolutionary Tree

Tarsier   Howler Monkey   Baboon   Gibbon   Orangutan   Gorilla   Human   Bonobo   Chimpanzee

Present

Millions of Years Ago

10

20

30

40

50

60

Prosimians

New World Monkeys

Old World Monkeys

Hominoids

Common Ancestor of Apes and Humans

Common Ancestor of Humans, Bonobos, and Chimpanzees

Common Ancestor of Primates

Look again at the hominoid branch on the primate evolutionary tree. The amount of difference between the DNA of humans and different apes tells you the *order* and *time* of species branching events. Notice the two lineages that split from an apelike ancestral population about 5 to 7 MYA. What species did each lineage produce?

Our Hominid Ancestors

Now let's look at the lineage that produced human beings (p. 103). This lineage is called the *hominid* (or hominin) family. Unlike apes, which walk on all fours, hominids walk upright on two legs (they are bipedal). What do you notice about this lineage? Why do you think it is called an evolutionary tree?

Scientists have used fossilized bones and teeth to reconstruct our family tree, but it isn't easy. Since hominids have been evolving as a separate group for only 6 million years, the fossil record is not very long and the differences among fossils are not always obvious. This

	Percent DNA That Is the Same as Human DNA
Gibbons	> 95%
Chimpanzees	> 98.3%
Bonobos (pygmy chimpanzees)	> 98.3%

Difference between Human DNA and Ape DNA

means that different scientists sometimes interpret the fossil record differently. Because of this, our knowledge of human evolution is tentative and subject to change. As new fossils are found, our understanding of human evolution improves.

For example, in 2002, scientists found a 6–7-million-year-old hominoid skull in the central African country of Chad. This early date is right around the time when scientists think that an ancestral hominoid population gave rise to both the chimp and hominid lineages. The shape of the skull and the teeth of the Chad fossil, called *Sahelanthropus tchadensis*, suggest to some scientists that it is one of the earliest members of the human family. Others think that it is an early member of the chimp lineage or perhaps the older gorilla lineage. Only more fossil finds will decide the issue. Scientists might, for example, find leg bones that show the creature walked upright and was therefore a hominid. If so, this would be the oldest hominid found to date. What does the discovery and interpretation of the Chad skull tell you about the nature of science?

Modern humans are just one of many hominid species that have evolved during the past 6 million years.

A simplified view of the hominid and chimpanzee lineages

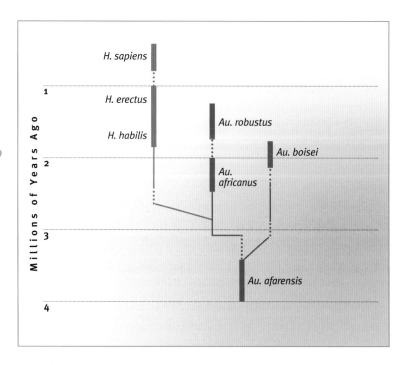

One hypothesis from the 1980s, based on fossil finds at the time

With this in mind, look at what scientists knew about the hominid fossil record when this book was published in the 1980s. How many hominids are there in the fossil record? When did the first hominid evolve? Did each hominid live at a different time or did they sometimes coexist? How long did different hominid species exist? How has the number of hominds in the fossil record changed across time?

Despite uncertainties about the status and classification of some fossils, scientists have established many facts about hominids. For example, over the past 6 million years, the hominid lineage has diversified into a branching tree of its own. By looking at the fossil record, scientists have concluded that the hominid tree contains many species (perhaps 16 or more) that overlapped in time and lived alongside one another. All of these species have become extinct except one—our own species, *Homo sapiens*.

Furthermore, the oldest hominid fossils are found in Africa. The oldest fossil generally agreed to be a hominid, *Ardipithecus ramidus* from Africa, is 5.5 million years old. Earlier fossils such as the Chad skull and *Orrorin tugenensis* exist, but scientists do not agree on whether they are hominids. Hominid fossils first appear outside of Africa nearly 2 million years ago. The early presence of hominids only in Africa is consistent with the hypothesis that humans originated in Africa. Studies of DNA diversity among modern peoples of the world also support this conclusion.

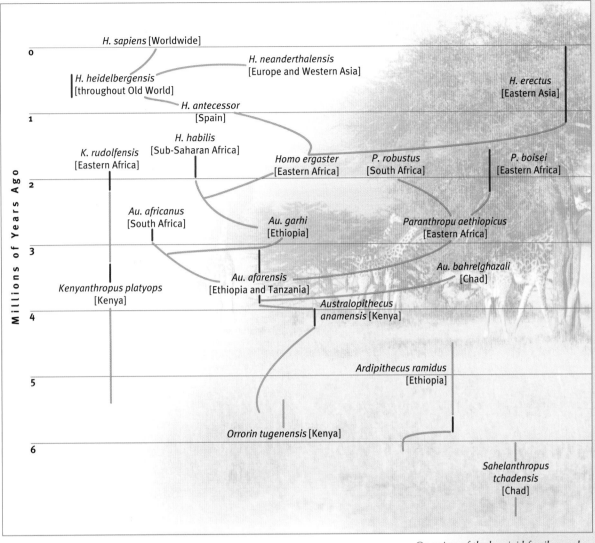

Overview of the hominid fossil record.
The blue lines represent the dates of
various hominids in the fossil record.
The orange lines represent proposed
evolutionary relationships among
hominid species.

From *Australopithecus* to *Homo*

Look again at the hominid fossil record. When did the genus
Australopithecus first evolve? *Australopithecus* evolved in Africa,
and scientists have identified at least eight australopithecine species.
Australopithecines walked upright like humans, although probably
not as gracefully. How do scientists know this? They can tell by
the structure of the skull, pelvis, backbone, and leg and foot bones.
Furthermore, in Tanzania, the footprints of two upright walkers
are preserved in hardened volcanic ash that is 3.7 million years old.
Unlike apes, the big toes are in line with the other toes just like in
humans. They had small brains like those of chimps, however.

The best known australopithecine is Lucy, a 1-meter- (3-foot-)
tall female *Australopithecus afarensis* who lived about 3.2 MYA.

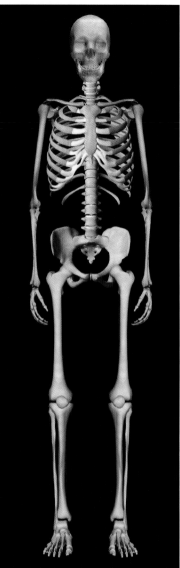

The skeletons of Lucy (left, a reconstruction) and an average modern female human (right) show that both walked upright on two legs. Notice the relative differences between the skeletons' arms, legs, and skulls.

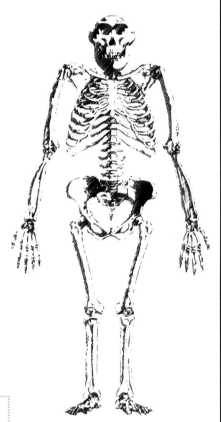

Lucy's skull, jaw, some of the teeth, limb proportions, fingers, and toes are apelike, but her legs, feet, and pelvis are more humanlike.

Plant and animal fossils found in the same locations as *Australopithecus* fossils indicate that they lived in woodlands and open grasslands with scattered trees, not in dense forests. They likely foraged upright on the ground, using their hands to gather plant food. Their teeth were adapted for eating tougher plant food such as nuts, grains, and hard fruits rather than soft forest fruits. Their curved, chimplike finger bones suggest that they were good at climbing trees.

Becoming Bipedal

Because most primates move along the ground on four limbs, scientists assume that the last common ancestor of humans and chimps (our closest relative) also moved around on all fours. How do you think upright walking came about? Complete the Take Charge of Your Learning task before you continue reading.

Scientists have proposed several hypotheses to explain the origin of bipedal movement. For example, one scientist proposed that two-legged movement evolved because it freed the arms to carry food and children. Another suggested that it originated as a feeding posture that provided access to food that had previously been out of reach. Still another hypothesized that it allowed early hominids to better regulate their body temperature because it exposed less body surface area to the hot African sun. What evidence would support or refute each hypothesis?

Another idea is that upright walking evolved in our ancient ancestors because it is a more energetically economical way to move around. Consider the following facts. Decide whether each fact is evidence for *or* evidence against the following hypothesis: Upright walking resulted from natural selection acting to improve the foraging efficiency of primates living in open environments.

- Chimpanzees expend more energy moving at walking speeds than humans of the same size.

- Early hominids evolved in open woodland and grassland environments where food is scattered in patches across vast distances.

- Chimps and other apes live in dense forests and do not have to move long distances to find food.

- Modern human hunter-gatherers often travel 10–13 kilometers (6–8 miles) a day in search of food.

- Africa's climate became drier between 1.8 million and 5 million years ago, causing forests to give way to open grasslands.

Natural selection has shaped humans in many other ways too. One controversial hypothesis is that natural selection caused various human skin colors to evolve. What evidence do you think scientists have for and against this hypothesis? Zoom in on the evolution of skin color to find out.

Around 2.5 MYA, the genus *Homo* branched from an unknown australopithecine population (possibly *Australopithecus africanus*).

Zoom in on a closer look at the evolution of human skin color.

The earliest *Homo* species are *Homo rudolfensis* and *Homo habilis* (1.8 to 2.5 MYA) from east Africa. Soon thereafter, *Homo ergaster* and *Homo erectus* appeared on the scene, although some scientists consider them to be the same species. Also appearing were several robust hominids (*Paranthropus*) whose massive jaws and grinding teeth were adaptations for eating tough, fibrous plants. Like many other hominid genera, this one became extinct.

The genus *Homo* was beginning to resemble modern humans. Compared with its australopithecine ancestors, *Homo* had a larger and rounder skull, a flatter face, smaller teeth, and more delicate jaws. Members of this genus also made stone tools, ate more meat, and later used fire. The genus *Homo* also had a larger brain than its predecessors. For example, at 820 cubic centimeters (50 cubic inches), *Homo erectus*'s brain was twice the size of an australopithecine's, and slightly more than half the volume of a modern human's brain (1,400 cubic centimeters [85 cubic inches]). Scientists know this by measuring their skulls.

Out of Africa . . . and Beyond

About 1.7 MYA some *Homo erectus* (or possibly *Homo ergaster*) left Africa in a first wave of migration and spread to Asia and eastern Europe. What became of them?

The fossil evidence shows that in Asia they became extinct. In Europe and the Middle East, they eventually evolved into Neanderthals (*Homo neanderthalensis*). These short, heavyset people used stone tools and buried their dead. They became extinct around 30,000 years ago.

What became of the *Homo* populations that stayed behind in Africa? Between 150,000 and 200,000 years ago, a stay-at-home African *Homo erectus* or *Homo ergaster* population eventually evolved into modern humans, *Homo sapiens*. Scientists have dated the origin of modern humans by comparing the mitochondrial DNA of people living in different parts of the world. Mitochondria are structures within cells that produce high-energy molecules (ATP) and contain tiny amounts of DNA that mutate at a constant rate across time.

The comparisons show that the total amount of variation among all people is small. This suggests that not much time has passed since modern humans originated. Calculations indicate the time of origin is within the past 200,000 years. Furthermore, Africans have more variation present than other populations. This suggests that

The human evolutionary tree has many branches. Modern humans represent the only branch that still exists.

they are the oldest population of modern humans and their ancestors were the first modern humans. Comparisons of the amount of genetic diversity among human populations today suggest that the first population of modern humans contained only 2,000–20,000 individuals. All 6 billion people living on Earth today are descendants of these individuals.

Molecular and fossil evidence show that 50,000–100,000 years ago, some of these large-brained, dark-skinned modern humans left home too—in another wave of migration from Africa. By 35,000 years ago, their descendants had spread widely throughout Australia, Asia, and Europe. In fact, these newcomers may have been responsible for the extinction of the Neanderthals already in Europe. By 15,000 years ago, modern humans had reached North America.

All humans are very similar to each other genetically.

We humans have our roots in Africa. Today's Africans are the descendants of the humans who stayed in Africa. People in the rest of the world are descended from the humans who left Africa. This common origin explains why all people in the world are much more similar to one another genetically (99.9 percent) than they are different.

"Humans may be the world's most dominant evolutionary force."

Stephen R. Palumbi,
Stanford University biologist

Humans as an Evolutionary Force

You have just learned that evolution affects humans. Now let's look at how humans affect the evolution of other species. As you read, use your knowledge to explain how evolution is occurring in the following situations.

Hunting

Most, but not all elephants, grow tusks made of ivory. Occasionally, elephants are born that do not grow tusks. These elephants have a mutation that prevents tusk growth. Scientists report that the percentage of tuskless elephants in Uganda has increased from 1 percent in 1930 to 25 percent in recent years. Poachers are killing elephants with tusks and selling the tusks on the black market.

How does this situation illustrate that evolution is occurring? How does it illustrate that humans are an evolutionary force?

Fighting Pests

In 1939, scientists discovered that the chemical DDT killed pest insects that were eating farm crops. Farmers began spraying their fields to protect their crops from these insects. By 1948, houseflies had become resistant to DDT. By the 1990s, more than 500 insect species had become resistant to at least one insecticide. Some of these species are so resistant that they are almost impossible to control. The same is true for herbicides (chemicals that kill weeds). Weed plants have become resistant to seven widely used herbicides in 25 years or less.

How do you think pesticide-resistant insects and plants arise? How do these situations illustrate that humans are an evolutionary force?

Fighting Disease

In the battle against disease-causing microorganisms, humans are in an evolutionary arms race. Scientists report that treating infections with antibiotics has favored the evolution of antibiotic-resistant bacteria. The only way to kill these bacteria is to increase the dosage or use a different antibiotic.

For example, nearly all disease-producing gram-positive bacteria in the 1940s were killed by penicillin. (Gram-positive bacteria are a large group of bacteria that have a certain type of cell wall.) Today, many of these bacteria are resistant to penicillin.

To kill penicillin-resistant bacteria, scientists developed the antibiotic methicillin. After bacteria became resistant to methicillin, they developed the antibiotic vancomycin. After bacteria became resistant to vancomycin, they developed the antibiotic Zyvox. This all occurred within a human lifetime. In fact, bacteria have evolved resistance to 10 different antibiotics in less than 40 years. Resistance to methicillin arose in just one year!

HIV (the human immunodeficiency virus) is the virus that causes AIDS (acquired immunodeficiency syndrome). The genetic makeup of this virus changes quickly within a person because of mutations. These mutations can cause the virus to become resistant to an antiviral drug within two weeks.

How do you think antibiotic-resistant bacteria and antiviral-resistant viruses evolve? How do these situations illustrate that humans are an evolutionary force?

Mining

When people mine Earth for minerals, they accumulate soil that has high concentrations of certain minerals. Scientists have discovered that plants growing on soil from zinc and lead mines can tolerate high concentrations of these metals. Plants of the same species growing just a few feet away on uncontaminated soil *cannot* tolerate high concentrations of these metals.

The following graph shows the zinc tolerance of plants collected near a zinc mine. Which plant samples were collected from zinc-contaminated soil? Which were taken from uncontaminated soil? Where is the boundary between the contaminated and the uncontaminated soils? How do you think zinc tolerance evolved in this plant? How does this situation illustrate that humans are an evolutionary force?

Index of Zinc Tolerance

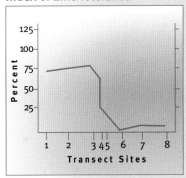

Zinc Tolerance in Plants

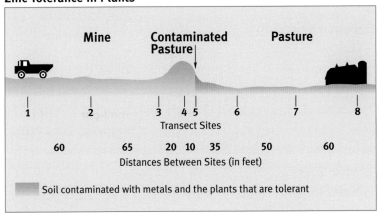

Selective Breeding

Look carefully at a pet dog. How is it different from a wolf? How is it similar? How do you explain these differences and similarities? Why are there so many varieties (breeds) of dogs?

Pet dogs and cats, cattle, sheep, goats, corn, and many other domesticated species are living examples that humans are an

Zoom in on the evolution of dogs.

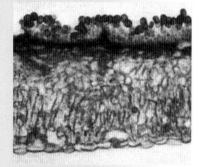

Humans produced dachshunds (top) and beagles (bottom) through the process of artificial selection.

Wheat rust is a fungus disease in wheat. This photo shows the fungus cells growing on a wheat leaf. The fungus absorbs nutrients from the plant's cells, which harms the plant.

evolutionary force. Humans produced them by controlling their reproduction while keeping them in captivity. How does the domestication of dogs illustrate evolution? How does it illustrate that humans are an evolutionary force? What needs or aspirations do people meet by domesticating species?

Humans used to survive by hunting animals and gathering wild plants. About 10,500 years ago, humans took up farming after they began controlling the evolution of several wild plant and animal species. Humans bred these species for traits they found useful. These traits include faster growth, bigger size, greater resistance to disease, more desirable body form and color, and better behavior.

Today, plant breeders are continuously breeding new varieties of wheat that are resistant to fungus attack. Unfortunately, fungi are constantly evolving ways of overcoming the wheat plant's resistance to attack. How does the wheat-fungus example illustrate evolution? How does it illustrate that humans are an evolutionary force?

Darwin talked a lot about artificial selection (that is, selective breeding or domestication) in his book *On the Origin of Species* because it was a model for natural selection. The difference between artificial selection and natural selection is in what does the selecting. In artificial selection, humans determine who or what reproduces and who or what does not. In natural selection, the environment influences who or what reproduces and who or what does not.

Genetic Engineering

Humans can genetically engineer species by inserting the genes from one species into the chromosomes of another. For example, scientists have put human genes into goats to make them produce a human blood-thinning protein in their milk. Scientists harvest the protein from the milk and use it to prevent blood clots in humans. Scientists have also placed fish antifreeze genes into tomatoes to make them more resistant to frost.

Scientists have created a variety of corn (called Bt corn) that is resistant to attack by the European corn borer beetle. They made it resistant by putting some genes from the bacterium *Bacillus thuringiensis* into the corn's DNA. These genes cause the corn's cells to produce enzymes that kill the beetle when it starts eating the plant. The genes enhance the plant's chances of survival and are passed on to the plant's offspring.

In fact, scientists have now identified more than 100 bacterial genes that kill insects. They are inserting these genes into many types of plants to protect them against pests. Other plants are being genetically engineered so that scientists can change their color, size, nutritional quality, ripening time, and other characteristics.

How does the Bt corn example illustrate evolution? How does genetic engineering illustrate that humans are an evolutionary force?

Humans Affecting Themselves

Besides affecting the evolution of other species, humans affect their own evolution too. During the past 10,000 years, lifestyle changes have affected the frequencies of enzymes that metabolize milk in some human populations. These populations have evolved the ability to digest milk as adults.

Nearly all human infants around the world can digest milk. This is not true for adults. In some populations, people lose their ability to digest milk during late childhood because their intestines stop producing lactase. Lactase is the enzyme that breaks down the main sugar in milk (lactose). In other populations, people keep producing lactase into adulthood. Lactase production is genetically determined. People who produce lactase throughout their lives have a different set of alleles than people who do not.

The following table shows the percentage of adults who can digest milk in various populations. Why do you think these differences exist?

A corn borer beetle attacking a corn plant.

Human activities affect the evolution of other species. Humans are affecting their own evolution too.

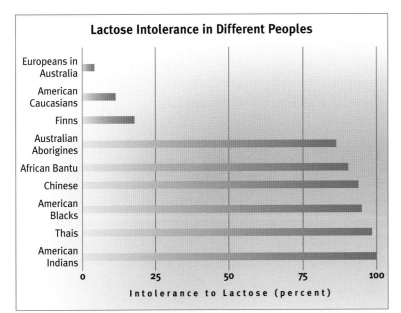

Lactose Intolerance in Different Peoples

The Masai tribe in Africa has long been associated with raising cattle. Unlike most African populations, adult Masai can digest milk.

Scientists have discovered that milk-digesting populations have a long history of drinking cattle, goat, or reindeer milk. This history dates back nearly 8,000 years to when some human populations began domesticating dairy animals. Before domestication, humans drank very little milk. Scientists calculate that it took only 400 generations for the frequencies of milk-digesting alleles to reach their current levels in milk-drinking populations.

The Cost of Being an Evolutionary Force

Our ability to influence the evolution of other species costs us money. For example, it costs about $80 million to develop a new pesticide and about $150 million to develop a new drug. Around $1.2 billion is spent on respraying agricultural fields. Another $2 billion or more is lost to pesticide-resistant organisms that eat human food crops. Increased drug payments and hospitalization required to treat drug-resistant diseases costs at least $30 billion. The total cost of human-induced evolution in the United States is estimated to be $33 billion to $50 billion per year, although it probably exceeds $100 billion a year. Luckily, scientists are discovering ways of slowing down evolution in other species. For example, doctors prescribe powerful new drugs only when infections cannot be treated with older drugs.

Now that you have learned that humans are an evolutionary force, go back and look at the quote by biologist Stephen Palumbi. Do you agree with him or not? What evidence supports your opinion?

Misconceptions about Evolution

Can you remember a time when you told a friend something, but later found out that she or he misunderstood you? Misunderstandings can have negative consequences.

People have misunderstandings about scientific theories too. We call scientific misunderstandings misconceptions. Misconceptions often occur because people get confused about concepts. Misconceptions in science are common because science can be complicated, so complete understanding is difficult to acquire. For example, the theory of evolution requires you to understand many interrelated concepts.

Let's look at several misconceptions people have about evolution and why it is important to avoid misconceptions. As you read, consider your own understanding. Do you have any of these misconceptions about evolution?

TAKE CHARGE ●
OF YOUR LEARNING

What is a scientific theory? What misconception do some people have about theories in science?

Misconception: The Inheritance of Acquired Traits

Recall Darwin's discovery of evolution by natural selection. Darwin lived during a time when people's scientific understanding of evolution was just beginning to unfold. Nearly 60 years before Darwin published his work, a naturalist named Lamarck tried to explain evolution with a different hypothesis.

Lamarck believed that *individuals* could evolve. He also thought that the traits an individual acquired during his or her lifetime were passed down to the next generation. For example, Lamarck thought that if people developed big muscles doing their jobs, their children would inherit their big muscles. While this might sound silly to us today, in Lamarck's day, scientists did not know about genetics.

What if our scientific understanding of evolution and genetics had not grown? Would it matter if everyone thought Lamarck's explanation for evolution was true? What if scientists had not worked out an understanding of inheritance that was more accurate than Lamarck's? How might that misconception have influenced your life?

Imagine for a moment that you dream of your children becoming professional athletes. To help make this happen, you take steroids to enlarge your muscles in the hope of passing this trait to your future offspring. What might be the consequences of this belief?

Disappointment and possible illness are consequences of believing that you can pass such an acquired trait to your offspring. Your misconception about the way evolution works will result in your being disappointed when your children do not inherit enlarged muscles. This misconception might also cause you to suffer from steroid-related liver disease or even cancer. As you can see, misconceptions about evolution can have serious consequences.

You might be thinking that Lamarck's ideas about evolution are hard to believe. After all, in Chapter 2 you read about scientists who investigated a physical trait and disproved Lamarck's ideas. First, they cut the tails short on adult mice. They then bred the mice with each other. All of their offspring had long tails. It was clear that the next generation did not inherit the acquired, short-tail trait. Yet some people today still have the misconception that offspring inherit their parents' acquired traits.

Read the following statements to see if you can identify the one that is consistent with Lamarck's ideas and the one that is consistent with Darwin's theory of evolution.

1. Some predators (such as cheetahs) chase down their prey (such as gazelles). Individual prey animals vary in their maximum running speed. Maximum running speed is an inherited trait whose upper limit is set by an individual's genes. Predators capture slower-running prey more often than faster-running prey. The faster-running survivors pass their genes for greater maximum running speed to their offspring through inheritance. As a result, future generations of prey are faster runners.

2. Some predators (such as cheetahs) chase down their prey (such as gazelles). Maximum running speed is an inherited trait whose upper limit is set by an individual's genes. Predators capture slower-running prey more often than faster-running prey. Individual prey animals strive to avoid predators by running faster, which increases their maximum running speed. They pass this speed increase to their offspring through inheritance. As a result, future generations of prey are faster runners.

Can you identify the Lamarckian ideas in one of the statements? See if you correctly identified the error in statement two. Individuals do not evolve, only populations evolve. Individuals cannot change their genetic makeup in response to environmental challenges. Individual cheetahs, for example, might become faster runners and approach their genetically limited maximum running speed through practice, but they cannot change genetic limits and pass this acquired improvement to their offspring through inheritance. Traits such as faster running acquired by training and stronger arms acquired through weight lifting cannot be inherited.

Lamarck did not know enough about inheritance to see that misconception in his explanation for evolution.

Misconception: The Biggest Is the Fittest

Now consider another common misconception. You have likely heard that natural selection is all about the "survival of the fittest." What does it mean to be fit? Do you think of something such as wild rams butting heads to see who is strongest? Many people think of an image like that when they think of evolution. They mistakenly think that the biggest individual is the fittest. How might that misunderstanding lead a person to make a bad choice in everyday life?

Border collie

Imagine that a friend decided to show and breed her favorite dogs, border collies. She owns a champion female that she raised from a puppy. The pup is now an adult, and your friend is looking for a male to father the dog's puppies. Your friend wants a *fit* male because she is going to show her collies in sheep- and cow-herding competitions.

At just the right time, she finds the male border collie she is seeking. He is the biggest border collie on his breeder's ranch. He has big bones and looks like he would hardly care if a cow kicked him. Your friend's female border collie is bred to this fine, *fit* male and she becomes pregnant. She grows large with puppies. In nine weeks, labor begins and your friend waits anxiously for the first puppy to be born. Several hours pass, and your friend's champion is laboring in pain. She rushes her dog to a veterinarian. The veterinarian examines her collie and takes your friend aside. "She can't deliver the puppies," he says, "they are too big. We'll have to perform a Caesarean section to get the puppies and save her life." But the surgery is difficult, and your friend's collie is exhausted. Your friend might lose her dog and the puppies. Suddenly, being the biggest is not necessarily the fittest.

Can you think of other examples where the biggest individual in a species is less fit than one who is medium or small in size? Domestic plants offer some good examples. Gardeners and farmers breed some flowers, like large dahlias, to be so big that they require wire supports to keep them from falling to the ground. Similarly, researchers bred varieties of oats to produce more grain and found that they blew down easily in high wind. The key idea is that *fittest* means best suited to survive and reproduce. The biggest is not necessarily the fittest.

A dahlia flower

Are the fittest individuals in a population decided by chance? At this point, you should know that natural selection is not random. The fittest individuals have traits that better adapt them to the environment. These individuals contribute more offspring to the next generation than individuals who are less well adapted.

Misconception: Evolution Occurs for the Good of the Species

Some people believe that traits evolve for the good of the species. *They don't.* Traits evolve because they promote the reproductive success of individuals. Most traits that benefit individuals also happen to benefit the species, but some do not. Some traits benefit the individual at the expense of the species, yet are common and favored by natural selection.

Consider a behavioral trait such as infanticide—the killing of infants. Infanticide is a disturbing and puzzling behavior that has been observed in at least 30 animal species, including lions, gorillas, insects, and birds. In some species, the infant-killers are male; in others, they are female.

For example, gorillas typically live in stable family groups made up of an adult male, several adult females, and their offspring. If the resident male dies, free-roaming bachelor males often attack and kill healthy nursing infants. In fact, bachelor males sometimes attack infants even when the resident male is around!

Scientists have observed that at least 37 percent of all infant gorilla deaths in the wild are caused by infanticide. In fact, most female gorillas have had at least one of their infants killed by a bachelor male. Females try to prevent the killing, but they are too small to put up much of a defense. Once a female's infant has been killed, she often leaves her existing group to go live with the killer and have her next baby with him.

If people think that traits evolve for the good of the species, how do they explain infanticide in so many species? How could the killing of healthy infants be good for a species?

Infanticide is not good for a species, but it is good for individuals. Infanticide in gorillas and other species has evolved because it enhances the killer's reproductive success. Recall that individuals with higher reproductive success are naturally selected. When a bachelor gorilla kills an infant, he wipes out his competitor's genetic contribution to the next generation and brings the dead infant's mother into reproductive readiness faster. This increases the killer's genetic representation in the gene pool at the expense of other males. Selection favors infanticide, as gruesome as it is, because it is adaptive for male gorillas to behave this way. That is, it promotes their reproductive success. Furthermore, it is adaptive for female victims of infanticide to go live with killer males because these males have demonstrated their power and aggressiveness. Such males potentially offer her next infant the kind of protection the previous male could not.

The Importance of Understanding Evolution

It is important for you to understand evolution accurately so that you can make important decisions that affect life on Earth. Think back to the examples you read in the section "Humans as an Evolutionary Force." The choices you make about things such as pesticides, antibiotics, land use, and genetic engineering will influence the evolution of humans and other species. Do you understand the theory of evolution well enough to make wise decisions?

● **TAKE CHARGE**
OF YOUR LEARNING

Explain why doctors need to understand evolution when treating AIDS.

In the Light of Evolution

Recall that biologist Theodosius Dobzhansky said that nothing in biology makes sense except in the light of evolution. Why did he say this? Because "seen in the light of evolution, biology is, perhaps, intellectually the most satisfying and inspiring science. Without that light it becomes a pile of sundry facts—some of them interesting or curious but making no meaningful picture as a whole." For this reason, Darwin's theory of evolution is the foundation of modern biology.

Like the other scientific theories you have read about in this book, such as the germ theory, scientists developed the theory of evolution to better understand the natural world, including human beings. To develop these theories, they thought scientifically. They made observations, asked questions about what they observed, collected evidence, and used that evidence to create a grand theory that explains why the living world is the way it is. You now understand that theory.

▪▪➡ **Activity:**
Biology in Light of Evolution

The theory of evolution is both simple and powerful. It says that all of the organisms we see today are the modified descendants of different types of organisms that lived in the past. This simple idea is powerful because it explains our observations about the living world.

Recall that since ancient times, people have been trying to explain the diversity, unity, and adaptations of life. The theory of

Biology makes sense only in the light of evolution.

biological evolution explains how Earth's dazzling variety of life (diversity) originated, why species have characteristics in common (unity), and why they are well suited to their environments (adaptation). It also helps us make sense of what we discover about the physiology, biochemistry, genetics, development, and behavior of organisms. In fact, it helps makes sense of everything we know about the living world.

The theory of evolution is scientific because it is based on evidence. This evidence includes the fossil record; the structural, embryological, and molecular similarities among species; the geographic distribution of species; the classification groups into which organisms fall; and direct observation. The theory also allows us to make predictions that can be tested through further observations and experiments.

New discoveries continue to support the theory of biological evolution, although it is constantly being refined. For example, Darwin thought that species change gradually across long periods of time. Recent fossil evidence, however, indicates that some species change little for long periods of time, then change rapidly over short periods. Such refinements mean that the theory is getting better at providing an evidence-based explanation for the living world. Although new discoveries lead to refinements, it is unlikely that fundamental parts of the theory (such as natural selection) will be overturned.

Do you want to test your new understanding of the living world? The next time you see a living organism, ask yourself the following questions:

- How is this species adapted to its environment?

- How is it different from other species?

- How is it the same as other species?

- How does my knowledge of evolution help me explain these adaptations, differences, and similarities?

- How did this species originate?

Do this a few times and you will be amazed by how much you can learn about the living world. Your journey of discovery is about to begin. ●

"Science is not only a way of knowing; it is also a way of discovering."

John A. Moore,
University of California biologist

References

Alles, D. L., & Stevenson, J. C. (2003). Teaching human evolution. *American Biology Teacher* 65(5), 333–339.

American Association for the Advancement of Science. (2001). *Atlas of science literacy.* Washington, DC: Project 2061 and the National Science Teachers Association.

Antonovics, J. (1971). The effects of a heterogeneous environment on the genetics of natural populations. *American Scientist 59,* 593–599.

Barash, D. (1977). *Sociobiology and behavior.* New York: Elsevier.

BBC News. (1998, September 25). Africa elephants "ditch tusks" to survive. *BBC Online Network.*

Benz, R. (2000). *Ecology and evolution: Islands of change.* Arlington, VA: NSTA Press.

Blair, D. (1998, September 24). Nature foils poachers as elephants shed tusks. *Daily Telegraph.*

Bybee, R. W. (Ed.). (2004). *Evolution in perspective.* Arlington, VA: NSTA Press.

Cann, R. L., & Wilson, A. C. (2003). The recent African genesis of humans [Special edition]. *Scientific American 13*(2), 54–61.

Diamond, J. (2002). Evolution, consequences and future of plant and animal domestication. *Nature 418,* 700–707.

Dobzhansky, T. (1973, March). Nothing in biology makes sense except in the light of evolution. *American Biology Teacher,* 125–129.

Dobzhansky, T., Ayala, F. J., Stebbins, G. L., & Valentine, J. W. (1977). *Evolution.* San Francisco, California: W.H. Freeman and Company.

Eaton, S. B., Shostak, M., & Konner, M. (1988). *The Paleolithic prescription.* New York: Harper and Row, Publishers.

Eldredge, N. (1999). *The pattern of evolution.* New York: W.H. Freeman and Company.

Freeman, S., & Herron, J. C. (1998). *Evolutionary analysis.* Upper Saddle River, NJ: Prentice-Hall.

Futuyma, D. J. (1998). *Evolutionary biology* (3rd ed.). Sunderland, MA: Sinauer Associates.

Goldsmith, T. H., & Zimmerman, W.F. (2001). *Biology, evolution, and human nature.* New York: Wiley and Sons.

Jablonski, N.G., & Chapli, G. (2003). Skin deep [Special edition]. *Scientific American 13*(2), 72–79.

Leakey, M., & Walker, A. (2003). Early hominid fossils from Africa [Special edition]. *Scientific American 13*(2), 14–19.

Leonard, W. R. (2003). Food for thought: Dietary change was a driving force in human evolution [Special edition]. *Scientific American 13*(2), 62–71.

Mayr, E. (2001). *What evolution is*. New York: Basic Books.

Milus, S. (2003, February 15). Sibling desperado. *Science News 163*, 102.

Molnar, S. (1992). Human variation. Upper Saddle River, NJ: Prentice Hall.

Moore, J. A. (1984). Science as a way of knowing— evolutionary biology. *American Zoologist 24*, 467–534.

Moore, J. A. (1990). *Science as a way of knowing–VII: A conceptual framework for biology, part III*. American Society of Zoologists.

Morell, V. (1997). The origin of dogs: Running with the wolves. *Science 276*, 1647–1648.

National Academy of Sciences. (1998). *Teaching about evolution and the nature of science*. Washington, DC: National Academy Press.

Palumbi, S. R. (2001). Humans as the world's greatest evolutionary force. *Science 293*, 1786–1790.

Reilly, P. R. (2000). *Abraham Lincoln's DNA and other adventures in genetics*. New York: Cold Spring Harbor Laboratory Press.

Science news this week: African legacy: Fossils plug gap in human origin. (2003, June 14). *Science News 163*(24), 371.

Science news this week: Stone Age genetics: Ancient DNA enters humanity's heritage. (2003, May 17). *Science News 163*, 307.

Starr, C., & Taggart, R. (1992). *Biology: The unity and diversity of life* (6th ed.). Belmont, CA: Wadsworth Publishing Company.

Stringer, C. (2003). Out of Ethiopia. *Nature 423*, 692–695.

Tattersall, I. (2003). Once we were not alone [Special edition]. *Scientific American 13*(2), 20–27.

Tattersall, I. (2003). Out of Africa again . . . and again? [Special edition]. *Scientific American 13*(2), 38–45.

The timescale and phylogeny of hominids. (2003). *Nature 422*(6934), 787–929. Figure retrieved April 24, 2003, from http://www.nature.com/nature/journal/v422/n6934/ fig_tab/nature01495_F1.html

Weiner, J. (1994). *The beak of the finch*. New York: Vintage Press.

Wells, S. (2003). *The journey of man: A genetic odyssey*. Princeton, NJ: Princeton University Press.

Wilford, J. N. (2003, June 11). Fossil skulls offer first glimpse of early human faces. *New York Times*.

Wong, K. (2003). An ancestor to call our own [Special edition]. *Scientific American 13*(2), 4–13.

Photo Credits